To Jack,

I understand you are a "Queens Kid" — Hope you find enjoyment in my memories of Brooklyn!

Enjoy —

All my best —

Tom Schlichter

Other Tom Sabellico books

I Can See Clearly Now
Ryne Duren Talks from the Heart About
Life, Baseball, and Alcohol
By Ryne Duren with Tom Sabellico

The Black Aces:
Baseball's Only African-American
Twenty-Game Winners
By Jim "Mudcat" Grant with Tom Sabellico
and Pat O'Brien

Betcha I Can
My Gamble to Succeed
By Stu "The Source" Feiner
as told to Tom Sabellico

STORIES FROM THE STOOP

as told by
Tom Sabellico

aventine press

Copyright © 2015, Tom Sabellico
First Edition

Without limiting the rights under copyright reserved above,
no part of this publication may be reproduced, stored in or introduced
into a retrieval system, or transmitted, in any form or by any means
(electronic, mechanical, photocopying, recording, or otherwise),
without the prior written permission of both the copyright owner
and the publisher of this book.

Published by Aventine Press
55 East Emerson St.
Chula Vista CA 91911
www.aventinepress.com

ISBN: 978-1-59330-879-7

Library of Congress Control Number: 2015903676
Library of Congress Cataloging-in-Publication Data
Tom Sabellico/Stories From The Stoop

Printed in the United States of America

ALL RIGHTS RESERVED

Cover Design by J. Louis Technology, Inc.

DEDICATION

To my parents (Rose and James), brother (Robert), grandparents (Sisto, Maria, Michael and Carmela), aunts (Angie, Antoinette, Carmela, Connie, Jean, Josie, Millie, Myna, and Nellie), uncles (Al, Al, Frank, Jerry, Joseph, Louis, Michael, and Salvatore) and cousins (Anthony, Antoinette, Camille, Carol Ann, Christine, Frank, James, James, Jerry, John, John, Joann, Joseph, Kathleen, Libby, Louis, Marie, Marie, Mary Jane, Michael, Mickey, and Patty), for providing a lifetime of love and memories;

To my wife, Paula: the events related in this book all occurred before we met, but for over forty years you have been key in the creation of a loving environment so that our children may hopefully have similar great memories of their childhood;

To my children (Christopher, Gina and James), their spouses (Stephen and Casandra) and my grandchildren (Anna Rose, Kate, James, Natalie Rose, Cole Thomas, and Joseph and those to come): you are the real reason I wrote this book, so that you may always know who came before you, the sacrifices they made, the love they shared by giving, and the life they provided by living. Read it, cherish it, live it and pass it on.

To my two best childhood friends: Maria Milza, literally the girl-next-door, you were the prettiest girl in the neighborhood, and as I looked back at pictures of all the important moments of my childhood, it seems you were right by my side; and Johnny Chisefsky, without question you were the most athletically talented kid I ever saw; you excelled at every sport and at being a guy's best friend.

TABLE OF CONTENTS

RECIPE INDEX

This is the actual stoop which is the focus of the book. Standing, left to right, are Fred Sabatini, me, Ken Sabatini and my brother Rob, on the occasion of Rob's confirmation. Seated on the stoop, where he always seemed to be, was Mister Joe, Aunt Mary's father.

INTRODUCTION

A number of recurring visions reside within the folds of my brain. They are much more detailed than those random thoughts that come to me and then leave within seconds, having no deep meaning and leaving no impression. They are more than just memories of some insignificant moment that quickly flash through your mind; much, much richer than that. They constitute the DNA of my childhood, carrying markers that identify my family and heritage and, I believe, ultimately come to define me.

The visions I speak of are so established in my brain I know exactly where they reside, emotionally. They are in the lush areas of the mind's memory that are enriched by receptors of perception and emotion. It is an area of the brain that harbors the childhood of my life; a time when innocence reigned uncontested and desire was only restrained by limited knowledge and experience; a time

1

when troubles, which might have seemed large, were obviously relatively small because they fit within a parent's hug which served to ease and erase them.

Although I can't tell you the physical location within my brain where these visions and memories reside, I know exactly how to get there, which enables me to visit them from time to time when the whimsy, or the melancholy, hits me. Although most times I visit them, there are many times when they visit me, without any voluntary action or desire on my part. Those visits, especially the involuntary ones, reaffirm my childhood experiences and continue to enrich me. While they exist only in my head, the visions and memories are so real they cause a visceral reaction within me. These mental film clips of a time in my past are so clear and repetitive that they must contain a message of import, something my inner being is drawing my attention to and forcing me to watch and observe.

If I manage to sit still long enough in a place that is quiet enough for my thoughts to be heard above the dog barking, the phone ringing, the beep of the microwave, the sound of an incoming text message, FedEx at the door and the other everyday noises of a busy household, my mind can take me on a more extended visit back to the streets of East New York, Brooklyn, in the 1950s and early 1960s. The scene is not always the street I grew up on (Essex Street), but it is clearly that neighborhood every time. Immediately I know where I am and in what direction I need to go to get back home.

There are many memories of special days, like Christmas, Easter, and First Holy Communion. And there are just as many memories of "ordinary" days, yet even those are extraordinary, rich with detail and emotion. Summer days at Rockaway Beach, a day at work with Dad in the "dark room" of the X-Ray Department, playing stoopball with my friends, Dad and a few friends playing polka under the streetlight because it was too hot inside with no air conditioning. And food played a big part in all of it too. Just like the combination of special days and everydays, the food memories could be of things that we only experienced once a year – like the Easter Meat Pie, Christmas pastries, or things that seemed to be staples of growing up as an Italian-American kid in Brooklyn – like the sauce Mom seemed to make every Sunday morning. Either way they are an important part of the memories of my childhood and as my mind's eye views these scenes from my past, my mind's nose inhales the familiar aromas and the sights and scents merge to transport me to places and times I cherish.

After my family moved from Brooklyn to Massapequa, Long Island, in 1966, among all the cultural changes I experienced I realized one huge difference. In suburbia every home had a backyard patio, and it was there that the neighbors congregated and spent their spare time. In Brooklyn, almost all of our families were apartment dwellers, and their favorite place to hang out was the front steps of the apartment building, an American urban phenomenon known as the "stoop." The stoop maintains a very revered place in the heart and memory of anybody who ever lived in the inner city, and especially Brooklyn. It was the safe area in front of your building. It was where you were allowed to play without your parents worrying about having to watch you. It was the playing field for stoopball. It was the "bench" while you waited your turn to play the winner in boxball. It was where you hung out and listened to the WMCA Good Guys or Cousin Brucie. It was where you escaped the heat of the apartment on a summer night, and begged to stay out late enough to see the stars come out. And most of all, it was a place where memories were both created and shared. The earliest relationships of our lives happened there, and, it was the place where the favorite stories of our parents, grandparents, aunts and uncles were handed down to our generation.

It is in honor of my family, my childhood friends and my neighborhood that I have written this book. I have related a good number of the stories I remember from my childhood. I am sure there are dozens more. I am also sure that many of the experiences I have recalled are similar to those experienced by my fellow Brooklynite Baby Boomers, and especially to those who grew up in Italian-American households. The comments I have received from those who have previewed the book, are that they felt I was writing about their family. That is how common many of our experiences were. <u>I would love to read your stories about your childhood and family and invite you to share them with me by visiting</u> **www.storiesfromthestoop.com**.

I find just the act of describing my childhood days as "the 1950s and early 1960s" very amusing, for that seems so long ago now, but the "60s" seemed so new and "cutting edge" then. Major League Baseball was expanding to California; a brand new team, the Mets, was coming to New York; NASA was launching men into orbit; television was being broadcast in "living color;" and the world came together at a Fair in Queens that gave us a peek at what futurists of the time thought the 21st Century would look like. So much has happened in my life and the world the fifty-odd years between then and now, yet it seems the majority of my richest memories were created between 1953 and 1966.

What could have happened in the years between my birth and age thirteen, and how special a place could East New York, Brooklyn, have been to cause me to make so many mental trips back to a time and place so distant and different from my current surroundings? Could it be the strong presence of family? Or the impact that religion played on my life at such an early age? The unbelievable closeness of childhood friends? Or the experience of coming of age? Or is it just that Brooklyn, for a variety of reasons, during those years was a magical place?

I have written this introduction before actually embarking on committing to writing my exploration of the time I spent living in East New York, Brooklyn, so I really don't know the answers to those questions yet. I may not know them when I reach the point when my mind has exhausted its memory bank of Brooklyn stories and remembrances. If that is so, then I will opt for magic as the answer. Again, I haven't started writing the story of this journey yet, but I have a strong feeling that the journey and the answer will both be somewhat magical. I hope you enjoy reading this book as much as I enjoy my mind's trips back to the old neighborhood. But I gotta go now. The guys are choosing up sides for stickball, and I just can't stand being picked last.

CHAPTER 1

COMING TO AMERICA

Where is the right place to begin my story of growing up in Brooklyn? At what moment in time, where, and why, were the wheels put in motion that made this a story worth writing and, more importantly to you, one worth reading? For many Baby Boomers like me who are "second-generation" Americans, the answers to those questions are: the turn of the twentieth century, somewhere in Europe, and the irresistible attraction of coming to America to explore new opportunities, respectively.

By the year 1900, the United States was still a relative newborn in the family of nations. Certainly its people had done their mightiest to catch up to its big sister countries around the world. Consider that within a period of just over a hundred years, America had declared its independence, waged and won a war for that freedom, settled a country clear across a continent, suffered its own Civil War, and had not only survived, but had grown to include 45 states and more than 76 million people. Impressive growth and activity to be sure.

The American experiment, centered around democracy and capitalism, was succeeding to such a degree, and conditions in Europe were such, that young Europeans, from country after country, were seeking to come to America to find the proverbial streets paved with gold. In many instances the immigrants did enjoy prosperity here, but it certainly wasn't guaranteed, nor immediate, or easy. In fact, when the stories are examined carefully, I offer that it was many of those immigrants who actually paved the streets in America, literally and figuratively. And if America had accomplished much in its first full century, all of that was about to be dwarfed by what America would experience in the next century, a century of growth, development, invention and change, that could not possibly have been predicted with any certainty, probably could not be understood if foretold, and is even hard to believe in retrospect.

I was born in Brooklyn in 1953, officially making me a member of the Baby Boomer Generation. We grew up with the development of television, the space program, and other inventions and developments too numerous to detail which identify my generation. Both of my parents were born in Manhattan, my mom in the Upper East Side (116th Street and Second Avenue) and my Dad in an area that was once part of Little Italy, but which has slowly become part of Chinatown, at 13 Mott Street. (As an indication of the cultural demographic shift, the local funeral director in the area back then was Charles Bacigalupo, at 26 Mulberry Street. That funeral parlor is now owned by Wah Wing Sang Funeral Corporation.)

Both of my parents came from Italian families, but with different backgrounds. My father's family always seemed to play a larger part in my childhood than my mother's family, and that may have been because of the sheer size of it, my dad being one of ten children. Also, the family was so close that all of my paternal grandparents' twenty-two grandchildren grew up as if we were brothers and sisters instead of cousins. Every one of my dad's brothers and sisters and their spouses treated me as if I were his or her own child, and my cousins and I treated our aunts and uncles with mutual respect. We listened to them as if they were our own parents. We knew they loved us and would never steer us wrong. The love among brothers, sisters, aunts, uncles, and cousins was amazing, as was the amount of time we all spent together. My mother's family was not as large and did not seem to make as deep an impression on me as a child. But the more mature version of me, looking backward, appreciates that the importance and the impact of my mother in my life is a reflection of the love and strength of her family.

My mother's parents were both born in this country and always seemed so much more modern to me than my paternal grandparents. In fact, I found it quite amazing what a difference being in this country one generation longer could make. But then again, my father's parents were more than a decade older than my mother's parents, and while I grew up with my mother's parents, who lived long enough to see me married and then some, I never had the honor of knowing or even meeting my dad's mother. She died the year before I was born. And my knowledge of my dad's father is mostly a collection of what I have been told by others. My personal recollections are only those from the mind and memory of a young child. He died when I was only a little more than five years old, but during that time I saw him every day and spent a lot of time with him since we lived in the same house.

Having represented many family members during my thirty-seven years as an attorney, I accumulated many documents, including birth and death certificates, marriage certificates, deeds and other assorted papers. It wasn't until I started digging through some of those documents that I realized my maternal relatives actually had more than a one generation head start in America over my paternal relatives. It appears from notes written by my mother's father, on an envelope containing the prayer cards from his in-law's respective wakes, that not only were he and my maternal grandmother born in this country, but so was his mother-in-law, Sinfarosa Schiaffo.

That knowledge made my impression of my maternal grandparents' modernism a little more understandable. My maternal great grandparents were only born a few years before my paternal grandfather, who was born in 1888. With the knowledge that one of my mother's grandparents was born in America, I wanted to know more about the details of the remainder of my ancestors' immigration to America. Growing up, I had no awareness of the story, although I did know they came here from Italy.

My maternal grandparents, Michael and Carmela (who everybody called Millie), shared the surname Cavallo before they were married. I remember repeatedly hearing the story during my childhood that when they wanted to marry they had to write to Rome to get a special dispensation from the Pope because their last names were the same. The story behind that was if they were related, the resultant inbreeding would create mentally retarded children, and since the Pope was infallible, his blessing would be taken as a sign that although they shared a common last name, marrying each other would not be a sin (or a medical liability) because they were not related. I never saw the letter that was supposedly sent to the Pope, and I never saw his response. I just took it on faith that no one was going to lie to me about anything having to do with the Pope, and I thought it was pretty cool that my grandfather had written to request the Pope's blessing to get married, and got it. (But I must confess that every time something a little weird happened on that side of the family, the thought immediately crossed my mind that the Pope might have made a mistake, or maybe they were pulling my leg after all about the whole dispensation thing.)

As I carefully read the documents my family members had entrusted to me, and used them as clues in researching the material available on the Internet, the background of my maternal grandparents and an explanation of the Cavallo surname developed. Among the documents was my maternal great-grandfather's Declaration of Intention to become a United States citizen. It was signed by him in 1932.

It contained some inaccuracies as to the name of the ship he came to America on (he came on the Phoenicia not the Proncio) and the date of his arrival (May 2, 1903, not 1902 as stated), which I was able to clear up with the help of the Ellis Island website. But more importantly the document contained historical biographical information about him and his wife, and my grandfather's family. My mother's paternal grandfather was born in Albanella, Italy, and the document states that my maternal great grandmother was born in Roccadaspide, Italy. As I checked the map of Italy, I discovered that although my mother always referred to her father's family as Napolitan (from Naples), the two towns of Roccadaspide and Albanella are actually south of

Salerno and Eboli, just off the famed Amalfi Coast, and midway between them lies a region known as **Cavallo**.

The Phoenicia's manifest for the trip leaving Naples on April 17, 1903 and arriving in New York on May 2, 1903, lists my great-grandfather, Francesco Cavallo, a "farm laborer," as one of 1,319 passengers. He is Passenger No. 23 on List MM. There were two other passengers on the same ship also named Francesco Cavallo. One was from Corleto Perticara, about 80 miles east of Albanella, and he was headed to Chicago, Illinois. The other was from Roccadaspide. He was a little older and listed Cincinnati, Ohio, as his destination. With my luck, chances are that the other two Francesco Cavallos were probably the ones with the money and we never heard from them again. Although I can't tell if my great-grandfather was related to the other Cavallos, a careful reading of the ship's manifest reveals that he was not travelling alone. He indicated that the relative he was going to join in America (his "sponsor"), was his brother, Michael Cavallo, at 340 East 113th Street, in Manhattan. The next three passengers on the list, Pasqual, Nicola and Luigi Guarracino, all listed their hometown as Albanella, all claimed they were "farm laborers," and all said the relative they were going to join was their brother-in-law, Michael Cavallo, at 340 East 113th Street, in Manhattan.

East 113th Street, Francesco Cavallo's intended destination in America, was in a neighborhood that was one of several Little Italies that sprung up in America at the turn of the century. Specifically, many of the immigrants who came from the area around Naples settled in East Harlem. So, I guess it wasn't a coincidence that two years after arriving in America, Francesco Cavallo, who lived at 324 East 115th Street, in East Harlem, married Rosa Scovotto, the proverbial girl-next-door, who had migrated there from the same area of Italy. Eleven months after their marriage, their first child, my maternal grandfather, Michael, was born on July 3, 1906. He was baptized at the Church of Our Lady of Mt. Carmel, the local parish, located at 449 East 115th Street.

Our Lady of Mt. Carmel is the most revered of religious icons among the Neapolitan people.

When Italians began to migrate to America in large numbers, they found that most Catholic churches had been established by the Irish, who were the earlier immigrants, seeking refuge from the potato famine in Ireland in the 1840s. Seeking the comfort that is found in familiarity, Italian immigrants established new parishes, honoring saints who were patron saints in their homeland. Immigrants felt most comfortable worshipping among their "own people" and also living among them, which explains the existence of Chinatowns, and Little Italies, and Germantowns. But on closer examination, within those enclaves created by country of origin, were smaller communities, divided by region. For instance, I came to learn in researching this book that another portion of East Harlem was home to many immigrants from Sicily, and within that community they established their own parish where they could worship together.

My mother's mother, Carmela, was born August 7, 1905, in Manhattan, and her name is a tribute to Our Lady of Mt. Carmel. She was also baptized at the Church of Our Lady of Mt. Carmel, and for those who think it is only a current practice for the Church to reach out to its parishioners in their native tongue, I offer you my grandmother's Baptism Certificate from the Chiesa della Madonna del Carmine (Church of Our Lady of Mt. Carmel) completely in Italian.

By 1924, my mother's maternal grandparents had moved from East Harlem to East New York in Brooklyn. Mike and Millie were married in a civil ceremony on January 26th, 1924, at City Hall, while they waited for the letter of dispensation from the Pope (a fact I only learned in researching this book – I had always been told they waited). They set up residence at 913 Lorraine Avenue in East New York, Brooklyn, and when the papal go-ahead finally came they got married in a religious ceremony at St. Rita's Church, in Brooklyn, on April 6, 1924. However, there was obviously still an attachment to East Harlem, since the reception was held at

Laurel Garden, 75 East 116th Street, in Manhattan. A year later, on October 16, 1925, Millie and Mike had their first child, my mom, Rose, named after her mother's mother, Sinfarosa, and her father's mother, Rosa.

The story was a little different on my father's side. Both of my paternal grandparents were born in Italy. My paternal grandmother died just before I was born. According to her Marriage Certificate, her name was Maria Giuseppa Ielardi, although there are discrepancies in that some documents list her name as Jerardi. She was born in Pisticci, in the province of Matera, in the region of Basilicata, in the southern end of Italy, just about seven miles north of the Mediterranean Sea. From the oral history I have been able to gather from my relatives, by all accounts, she was a wonderful woman with a generous heart, a knack for raising a family that loved and supported each other, and a fabulous ability to tell stories.

My memories of her have been created from two sources: the 8mm silent films my dad took with his Bell and Howell movie camera, and the stories my family has repeated whenever her name is mentioned or the movies are shown. I understand she was a hardworking woman who accepted a difficult situation in life, as you will come to see, and she had a natural, common-sense, intelligence. Faced with my grandfather's disability and resultant relative immobility, she did what she had to do to raise a family with the limited resources she had. She maintained a small flock of chickens in the side yard, which provided eggs for her table, and, on occasion, a chicken for dinner (much to my Uncle Sal's chagrin when he came home from school one day to find that his "pet" chicken was that night's dinner). She kept an eye out for wood, and had her sons saw it to the right size to keep the furnace stoked. I remember Uncle Frank telling me that she would go the local A&P with an empty cigar box to collect all the different grinds from the coffee machines that didn't make it into customers' bags, to use at home, and as a blend it made terrific coffee.

I have always been told that she was a great story-teller, and used her stories like parables to teach her children. She also had some favorite sayings she repeated to make a point and my dad and my aunts and uncles would repeat them to us, to teach another generation. The particular ones I remember, and also repeat to my children, are: "If you eat with two hands you choke yourself" (warning against greed and gluttony); "What you put you find. If you put chicken, don't expect to find steak" (stressing that your results will be defined by your efforts); "You buy cheap you buy twice" (which is self-explanatory); and my favorite: "Poor is not one who has little, but one who wants much" (which clearly defines for me why my family, though not financially well off, never, never considered themselves "poor").

What I observed from the films and photos I have seen of her was her warm, easy smile. What I observed from listening and watching her children and grandchildren was a reflection of the love she had for them and the way they all cherished her.

I am going to go out on a bit of a limb here with my theory about my paternal grandmother, and Italian mothers in general. It is a widely held belief, strengthened by books and movies, that Italian families are patriarchies, ruled by the all-knowing and all-powerful father (and "Godfather", thanks to Mario Puzo). However, I believe that the mother is a very strong figure in an Italian family. My observation is that inside the family, especially in the singular relationship between the husband and wife, the wife can be the strength of the family. And one of her most important strengths is to make it appear to the outside world that the husband, the father, is the head of the family, secure in the knowledge of her influence on her husband and her family.

My aunts and uncles and older cousins relate with a touch of amazement how my grandmother, who did not speak or write English, negotiated her way around New York on the subway system and did all she had to do for her family. My oldest cousin Antoinette tells me she would accompany Grandma to the cemetery to visit Uncle Angelo's grave, and she doesn't know how Grandma knew where to go. She also remembers going with Grandma, by subway, to feasts where my grandfather, Sisto, was trying to make money by selling pencils. If it was three stops on the train, Grandma would put three pebbles in her pocket to keep count of where she was going. My grandmother would gather all of the coins Sisto had collected into a red and white kerchief and take them home, to save Sisto from having to carry them, and probably to protect against Sisto spending or losing them. Later in the night Uncle Frank would go back and bring Sisto home.

My paternal grandfather came from Alatri, in the province of Frosinone, in the region of Lazio, outside of Rome. His name was Sisto Sabellico, one of the many children of Alatri named Sisto, in honor of their patron saint, Pope Sisto I. During the past ten or fifteen years I have met many people here in New York who claimed their ancestors came from Frosinone. In fact, mention of Frosinone to descendants of those from that region, seems to evoke a response similar to mentioning Brooklyn in this country. Maybe that is the start of the magic of Brooklyn.

Of all my grandparents' stories, Sisto's was a little different. Although it didn't involve the Pope, (except as his namesake), it was a little more emotional and lends its own magic to my background. Sisto was born in 1888. He was the first person I actually met and knew who was born in the 1800s. (Although I would have to believe that some of my earliest teachers, nuns of the Sisters of Saint Joseph, were his contemporaries.) At the age of 17, in 1905, he set sail for America on the *Napolitan Prince*.

The ship's manifest indicates the trip took nineteen days, leaving Naples on April 5th and arriving in New York on April 24th. My grandfather had all of $11 with him (which was worth a lot more then than now, but was still only $11), and had no family here to meet him. In what seems like a curious coincidence, or a case of the authorities winking and turning their heads, my grandfather and six other passengers on the ship all listed the same person here in America, Sisto Maggi, 71 Mulberry Street,

New York, as their "sponsor," although only one person, G. Battista Maggi, also from Alatri, indicated the actual relationship, his sponsor was his brother.

I'm not sure exactly what type of test my grandfather and his shipmates were exposed to on the *Napolitan Prince*, but the reverse side of the ship's manifest contains a sworn statement of the ship's Commanding Officer, H. Eagleton, that he **"caused the surgeon of said vessel sailing therewith, or the surgeon employed by the owners thereof, to make a physical and oral examination of each and all of the aliens named in the foregoing Lists or Manifest Sheets, 29 in number, and that from the report of said surgeon and from my own investigation, I believe that no one of said aliens is an idiot, or insane person, or a pauper, or is likely to become a public charge, or is suffering from a loathsome or a dangerous contagious disease, or is a person who has been convicted of a felony or other crime or misdemeanor involving moral turpitude, or a polygamist, or an anarchist, or under promise or agreement, express or implied, to perform labor in the United States, or a prostitute, and that also, according to the best of my knowledge and belief, the information in said Lists or Manifests concerning each of said aliens named therein is correct and true in every respect."** I just wonder about the effectiveness of that test. If every immigrant took the test and passed, how did we wind up with so many idiots, insane people, paupers, public charges, people with loathsome and contagious diseases, criminals, polygamists and prostitutes?

Sisto successfully made it to America, passing through the immigration inspection system in place at Ellis Island. Today, as the result of a Father's Day present I gave to my dad, Sisto Sabellico's name is listed on a plaque on Ellis Island, commemorating the fact that he was one of the immigrants passing through the historic gateway to the land of opportunity.

Sisto didn't stay in New York for long. Others who had come from his area in Italy had worked in the construction and mining industry in New England, and Sisto took off to join them.

The way the story came to me from my dad was that Sisto was sitting around a campfire after a hard day's labor, when one of the workers who still had dynamite in his shirt, from the demolition work they were doing, got too close to the fire. As a result of the explosion that took place, Sisto's leg was badly injured and cinders and debris caused serious scratches to his eyes, necessitating covering them with gauze. Hampered by being unable to communicate with the hospital staff because of the language barrier, dazed from pain and medication, and with his vision blocked, Sisto tugged and scratched at the pain in his leg, seeking relief from the burns he suffered, unaware of the additional damage he was causing. Gangrene set in and medical science being what it was in the early 1900s, the leg had to be amputated. No prosthesis existed at that time with any semblance of duplicating his leg, let alone any functions thereof.

The story I always heard from my dad was that Sisto was able to recover the sum of $5,000 for the damages he suffered, but the lawyer he retained to represent him (a Mr. Russo) took off with the settlement proceeds, all of it. That left Sisto as a young man of just under twenty, with one leg, in a foreign country, unable to speak English, and with no money. The thought of my grandfather's plight and the view of him afforded to me by my mind's eye, in that disadvantageous position, brings me to tears. I often think of the courage and sense of adventure he must have had, having set sail for a new world, full of the enthusiasm it would take to leave his family a world behind, and ready to conquer whatever he met. I would love to know what this teenager, who I only knew as a handicapped old man with a pipe, who spoke "broken" English, must have been thinking when he first came to this country. What emotion did he feel when he first saw the Statue of Liberty standing in the harbor welcoming him to America? What did he look like? How did he handle himself? How did he manage to find a way? I imagine his mood was probably a mixture of adventure, hope and great anticipation.

Then, just a few years later, he was without a leg, an education, a job or a foreseeable future, an ocean away from all that he considered familiar and comforting. What was he thinking then? How did he find the strength and the courage and the endurance to go on? For Sisto's descendants to have risen from his difficult beginning is a testimony to the love he and his wife instilled in his children, the legacy of the hard work performed by his family and the opportunities afforded by this great nation.

Although I had no reason to doubt Sisto's story as told to me by my dad, I was always curious to know how Sisto, who listed his job as an Organ Grinder and a Peddler on his Draft Registration forms, was able to purchase a two-family house in Brooklyn, which according to my dad was built and purchased in 1925. In writing this book I researched the New York City Register's records for the deeds of the Essex Street property and came to learn that in January 1912, Sisto purchased a 20' x 100' lot on Essex Street, and in 1915 he purchased an additional 40' x 100' lot, which together formed 688 Essex Street, between New Lots Avenue and Hegeman Avenue, in Brooklyn. I returned to the documents left to me by family members and there among the papers my Uncle Frank had given me, in an envelope I had never opened, was the original Deed for the 20' x 100' lot. Coincidentally, I found it on January 15, 2012, exactly one hundred years to the day after it was signed.

Over a number of years, somehow Sisto and Maria found the money to build a two-family home which they moved into in 1925, when my dad was one year old. It served as the Sabellico family homestead for over forty years, the site of many family events, only some of which were captured on film by my dad. It is the house where I was conceived (from what I was told) and lived during the first six years of my life. Maybe, just maybe, Sisto took his settlement proceeds and purchased those lots, with a view towards the future. Another possibility, considering that Sisto and Maria married in 1910, was that there was some dowry as a result of the marriage. At this point, I don't think I will ever know for sure.

While Sisto was in New England recovering from his injury and learning to cope with one leg, Maria Giuseppa Ielardi had made her way to America. She would not meet Sisto until after his accident. From what my dad told me, when they first met at a social function, Sisto would not sit down, because the prosthesis he was finally able to obtain, without a hinge, would stick out like a sore leg. When Maria next saw Sisto, without his prosthesis, she thought he had just suffered the loss of his leg. From that point forward, her love for this man, handicapped as he might have been, and their love for each other, grew.

They got married on December 10, 1910 at St. Joachim's Church on Roosevelt Street in Manhattan. (An interesting side note about St. Joachim's is that it was first established in 1888 [the year of Sisto's birth] for Italian immigrants seeking to worship at religious services in their native tongue, and the church was demolished in 1958 [the year Sisto died] as part of an urban renewal process.) Sisto and Maria set up house in an apartment in lower Manhattan and starting having babies – ten children in all, which always led my father to comment that obviously Sisto's missing leg wasn't the leg that was important in siring children. I heard that line since I was a little kid and eventually I understood it. When I did, I allowed myself to laugh, to myself. My Catholic school upbringing and fear of my father's response to anything I did off-color would never allow me to acknowledge that I understood the sexual reference in that comment.

Of Maria and Sisto's ten children, only one suffered ill health as a child, my father's older brother, Angelo, who died at ten months old, on June 22, 1921. I learned about my Uncle Angelo's death as a child when I first accompanied my dad to visit my grandparents' gravesite in Calvary Cemetery in Queens and saw Angelo's name on the tombstone. I remember asking my dad about it as I looked at the monument, and I distinctly recall his tear filled answer about how his brother had died as a baby.

Even though he had never known him, the love of the family was evident to me, in my dad's emotional response.

The remaining nine children, five boys and four girls, produced twenty-two grandchildren and over forty great-grandchildren for Maria and Sisto. Their oldest child, Frank, was born in 1911, and the youngest, Angelina, was born in 1932. In between, came Louis (1913), Josephine (1918), Angelo (1920), Joseph (1922), James (1924), Carmela (1927), Antoinette (1929), and Salvatore (1930). Uncle Frank sacrificed much in life as a young man to act as a second father to his siblings. I remember him telling me about leaving school to work as a shoe shine boy, and at other assorted jobs, to help the family, including putting the lights on for the family's Jewish neighbors on the Sabbath, earning nickels because the Jewish people could not perform those tasks on their holy day. He also served as an altar boy for The Transfiguration Church in Little Italy where the family lived until he was 14. Uncle Frank had seriously considered entering the priesthood, but he knew the family needed him more than the Church did. The family's respect for Uncle Frank was magnificent, and well-earned. Mostly through his efforts, this branch of the family was able to survive.

Meanwhile, the two separate and distinct Cavallo families, my maternal grandfather's parents and my maternal grandmother's parents, were also settling into New York, his on the upper east side of New York, and hers in East New York. I don't know how Mike the butcher, my maternal grandfather, met Millie, my maternal grandmother. What I do know from the stories I was told as a child, was that when they were newlyweds, Mike had his own butcher shop, and was doing well. Then came the Great Depression, and Mike couldn't resist the pleas of his customers to run a tab, accepting their scribbled IOUs and promises that they would pay him next week, or next month, or whenever. Eventually, from helping everyone else in trouble, he had to put a lock on the door to his shop. I am not sure exactly how my grandmother's parents accumulated whatever money they did, but they had enough to own two four-family buildings on Essex Street, 718 and 720. Eventually, they left 718 to my grandparents and 720 to Millie's brother, my Uncle Dominic and his wife, Mary. When I was six years old, after Sisto died, we moved into one of the apartments in 718, first floor, front. My best friend, Johnny Chisefsky, and his family moved into our old apartment at 688, and Maria Milza, (who was like Darla of the Little Rascals in my group of friends), lived at 720 and so did Uncle Sal and Aunt Jean.

So, from the Italian towns of Alatri, Pisticci, Roccadaspide and Albanelli, from the Upper East Side of Manhattan and from Little Italy, the elements of my ancestry moved until they were all aligned in Brooklyn, on the west side of Essex Street, between New Lots Avenue and Hegeman Avenue, just several houses away from each other. Essex Street was a one-way street, going south to north, with 718 being the more southerly. As my father has told me, one day in 1947, he was in the garden next to 688, with his dad, when Mike and Millie Cavallo's 21 year old daughter, Rose, went walking by. My dad asked my grandfather who she was, and Sisto's response was "Mike the butcher's daughter, never you mind." Dad's take on it was that his father felt there was an economic gap between the families. That, however, did not deter my dad, and nine months later, on April 3, 1948, my mom and dad were married by Father Hart at St. Fortunata's RC Church on Linden Boulevard in Brooklyn. St. Fortunata Church was another parish whose origin is traced directly to the desires of Napolitan immigrants to honor one of their own, while worshiping with their own. (In researching this book I learned that St. Fortunata was a virgin who, along with her three brothers, was martyred in Palestine, circa 303 AD, and whose remains were transported to Naples, Italy where they were revered for centuries before being transported to Baucina, a small province of Palermo, Italy, where they remain today. She is the patroness saint of Baucina, and her life is celebrated annually with a feast.)

688 Essex Street, Brooklyn, NY, in 1925, the year my grandparents moved in. The baby being held by my grandmother is my father who was one year old.

Grandpa Sisto at his "command center," the kitchen window of 688 Essex Street.

CHAPTER 2

SISTO

Of my four grandparents the one whose life stories always seemed to have been repeated the most, and always seemed to be most interesting, was my father's father: Sisto. As I have already stated, unfortunately I never had the opportunity to know my father's mother, and I truly consider that a loss from all I've heard. The fact that she doesn't occupy a larger part of my memory is a negative I cannot correct. I really wish that I could have interacted with her, felt her love, and learned about life at her side.

As for my mother's parents, they moved to Florida from Brooklyn, when we moved to Long Island. Although I obviously got to know them for a much longer period of my life, and I was blessed to have many memories of them, their lives seem, in my mind, to have been much less epic than that of Sisto.

I have already shared with you the story of his trip to America and the loss of his leg at a young age. Add to that his ten children and the way that his family grew and stayed together in love, and I think it, by itself, could be the topic of its own book. But to give you the right framework of my time in Brooklyn I think it is necessary to know some of what went before. The brief history I have shared of how my grandparents came to Brooklyn was an appetizer. Now consider the story of Sisto to be the first glass of wine we enjoy together before we delve into the meat of the story.

From my memory, and from what I have been told, Sisto was larger-than-life. A narrative of his life is not the rags to riches story that Hollywood has made famous. There was no winning lottery ticket, no rise from log cabin poor to Park Avenue rich. No headlines. No streets named after him. He didn't create a family fortune or establish a charitable foundation. He didn't attend college, or high school, or any school here in America. No, his life was not easy. In fact, if not for the love and companionship of my grandmother, he might not have survived, and if not for the sacrifices made and the loyalty and love shown by his oldest son, Frank, and the other children who followed his example, there might not be any stories to tell.

My statement that Sisto was larger-than-life is an obvious double entendre to those who actually knew him. My memory is that he was an extremely large man. My dad filled in the details for me, telling me that Sisto, who only had one leg, weighed well over 400 pounds, and had a 72 inch waist and a 22 ½ inch neck. His chest and upper arms were massive as a result of years of lifting his body weight on his crutches. I remember his presence. That was the physical part of his grandeur.

The quality of my memories of Sisto compensates for the lack of quantity.

The majority of the stories that have been told over and over about Sisto center on his love for life, his gusto, his down-to-earth persona that included a love for family, an appetite, and a temper. Earlier I wrote about my grandmother's favorite sayings. One of Sisto's which I quote quite often, and which I believe explains his philosophy of life, is "When you dance, dance."

His crutches, which along with his pipe were his constant companions, became a prop for Sisto. He used those crutches for a lot more than walking. He used them to bang against the steam pipe to get your attention. He used them to reach objects he couldn't otherwise get to without getting up. He used them to discipline his children and grandchildren. He used them as instruments of entertainment, holding one against his chin, and playing it with the other like a violin, emulating my Uncle Jerry (Santangelo) who actually could play the violin.

Although I was not yet six years old when Sisto died, I have distinct memories of him. From the day I was born until the day Sisto died, we lived in the same house. He lived downstairs, with Aunt Angie, Aunt Antoinette and Uncle Al (Taylor). My mom, dad, my brother, Rob, and I lived upstairs.

Sisto had a very harsh beard. He didn't shave on his own, only when one of his sons shaved him with a straight razor. Uncle Louie was the family barber. Dad said when Uncle Louie was going to shave Sisto's head everybody else in the house had to be quiet or leave, so as not to distract Uncle Louie. On the days in between shaves, Sisto's beard felt like very coarse sandpaper to a kid. And he gave us every opportunity to experience that. He would pick us up and rub our tender face against his beard and howl with laughter as we screamed in pain.

I remember his pipe, how he was never without it, how he chugged on it, and how it smoked. He would entice me with a shiny penny, and place it on the table just out of my reach. When I reached for it, he would move it further, until finally he would place it on the top of the bowl of his pipe. As a young boy, I didn't account for the heat of the pipe; I was just attracted by the shine of the penny. When I would reach for the penny, and then draw back my hand because of the pipe's heat, he would laugh and his belly would shake like jelly, just like the legendary St. Nick.

I have a clear memory of the scene right in front of 688 Essex Street, facing the stoop. Along the street there was a telephone pole and a sycamore tree, separated by about a four foot distance. (Thanks to Google Maps, I notice that the tree and pole still stand today.) Sandwiched between that tree and pole was a piece of cement that had been part of a stoop of another building. It was about three feet long and a foot and a half square. It served as Sisto's bench. Where many chairs had fallen to his weight, this slab of concrete was meant for him. It was his outside throne, from which he could see his kingdom: his house and his family – all he needed or cared about. Inside the house, Sisto sat at a chair located right by the kitchen window, enabling him to see the outside world. It was within a crutch's distance from the steam pipe, which served as his Flintstone-type intercom, when he needed my dad, or one of us, to come downstairs. He was way ahead of Tony Orlando and the knock three times on the pipe thing. His seat was basically at the kitchen table, and right near the stove and the kitchen sink. It was his internal command center.

When he wasn't in the kitchen or in front of the house, Sisto could be found in the living room in front of the television. I remember watching television with him, and how heartily he laughed at comedy shows, especially *I Love Lucy* and *Amos and Andy*, his favorites.

Those are memories I have, but they are not the tales which I have heard my relatives repeat until they became legend. These are just a few to give you a flavor of the man:

From 1919 to 1933, the manufacture, sale, and transportation of alcohol for consumption were banned nationally by the Eighteenth Amendment to the United States Constitution. This period was known as Prohibition. However, the National Prohibition Act, the legislation that introduced Prohibition did not outlaw the consumption of alcoholic beverages. Only the manufacturers and sellers were at risk. That meant there was still a thirsty portion of the population who could drink with impunity. In fact, in response to Prohibition, alcohol use became chic, and demand actually increased. The only problem was to find the wine, beer and alcohol the people craved. The market for alcohol was so great that the manufacture of alcoholic beverages as a cottage industry became a widespread activity. Authorities estimate that by 1930 the illegal production of alcoholic beverages was a $30 million dollar a year industry in America.

Following a business pattern that drove, and drives, the American economy, Sisto saw the need and knew that he had the talent, and heritage, to make wine, and he could figure out how to brew beer. It was in his blood. He simply made the wine his family had made, just more of it, to the extent that his main source of income in the years of the American Prohibition was the prohibited manufacture and sale of alcoholic beverages, namely: wine and beer. To use the terminology of the time, he was a bootlegger. My dad always laughed at the irony of it, when he described his father as a "one-legged bootlegger." And Sisto was not alone in his bootlegging endeavors. Almost every Italian family in the neighborhood was making wine, and learning how to brew beer, and according to my dad, the cops were the bootleggers' best customers.

The basement at 688 Essex Street became a brewery and in the very back of the basement was a door that led to a sub-basement, the wine cellar. I have no independent memory of the beer making, but I can still see, and smell, the wine cellar. It was a dark, mini-cave of a place, with three fifty-five gallon oak barrels lying on their sides to the right as you entered. It seems like the damp mustiness immediately attached to your clothing and everyone you came into contact with for the next hour or so knew that you had been in the wine cellar. As I got older, and Dad continued to make his father's wine for years, I remember sneaking into the wine cellar and opening that spigot for a stolen sip on more than one occasion.

Sisto's next door neighbor, Mike, ran his own mini-brewery down his basement, and Dad loved to tell the following story. One summer day, a neighborhood cop who was one of Mike's regular customers came by for a cold beer and Mike was not home. Putting his thirst above loyalty, the cop bought a bottle of beer from Sisto. When Mike found out about it, he made a big stink, calling Sisto some very unfavorable names. Sisto became irate, but as a man on crutches he couldn't strike out immediately but had to wait for his opportunity. A couple of days later, as Sisto sat outside on his concrete block, Mike rode by on his bicycle. Sisto hurled one of his crutches at him, and hit Mike square in the forehead, knocking him off the bike. Sisto hobbled over on his one remaining crutch and proceeded to beat Mike silly. Luckily for Sisto, the cops who showed up were his customers and they wrote up a report that Mike fell off the fence causing his facial injuries.

The making of home-made wine was a fundamental part of almost every Italian-American home in Brooklyn. The father of every family had his own recipe and his own "secrets" handed down to him, which made his blend of wine unique and special. It paralleled how families felt about their recipe for the Sunday tomato sauce – each family's recipe was similar yet somehow unique based on what their parents and grandparents taught them. I remember that after Sisto passed away Dad continued to make his wine in his honor and memory. Every fall we would drive to the Canarsie Terminal Market for the grapes. Based on his father's recipe, Dad would buy Muscato (for its high alcohol content), Cry Baby Alicante and Zinfandel. I remember him telling me that the Alicante was one of the few grapes whose juice was actually red, adding to the strength of the wine. I also remember trips to the Canarsie Terminal Market because of the specialty foods they had there: barrels of different types of olives, all kinds of cheeses (which they cut with a wire, which I thought was cool), and special Italian foods, like dried sausages, pepperoni, and Orzata. Orzata is almond flavored syrup. Mom would fill a pitcher with ice and water and add just enough of the sweet Orzata syrup to make it just perfect. Just saying the name I can taste the almond flavor, see the condensation running down the side of the pitcher and feel the heat of summer and the relief as the Orzata passes over my throat.

The older Italian men on Essex Street always found ways to amuse themselves; usually it was playing bocce or cards, or arguing about bocce or cards, or who made the best wine. In our neighborhood there was no formal bocce court. All the older Italian men would congregate at the undeveloped lot on Hegeman Avenue, between Linwood Street and Essex Street. The method by which they would choose sides was a war in itself. They engaged in an Italian game called *Morra*, which was "played" by two men, each starting with his fist clenched behind his back. As each man thrust his fist forward and put forth anywhere from zero to five fingers, he would call out his guess as to the total number of fingers put forth by him and his opponent. As a kid watching them you could learn to count to ten in Italian and you could learn some simple math (and some really cool Italian curse words). If you were playing and put out no fingers then the highest number you should call out is "Cinque!" (five), and if you put out any fingers at all you obviously could not call "Zero" (the same in both Italian and English). Once the war of choosing sides was completed the fun really started. If no one had a yardstick or folding ruler they would use a stick or broken branch to measure which team got closest to the pallino (the small ball). Boy, I can still hear the arguments, all in Italian, with hands flailing. I don't ever remember seeing women play bocce back in Brooklyn.

The card games could get just as heated. They would play either Scopa or Brišc (formally known as Briscola). Both of these games were played using an Italian deck of cards, or a poker deck, taking out the 8s, 9s and 10s. Both games could be played one-on-one, but were usually played in teams of two against each other, which lent itself to an extensive system of signals and allegations of cheating, which, fueled by the consumption of wine, escalated the tensions and the voices.

After the playing was over the serious drinking would begin, but boys being boys that was also a competition. The captain of the winning team would be the Boss and the captain of the losing team would be the Underboss, and all the men would play a game called Padrone e Sottopadrone (Boss and Underboss). They would pour out enough drinks for everyone, and the game would start with the Boss making a proposal to the Underboss: a drink for me, a drink for you, and a drink for everyone on my team. Of course, that would be unacceptable to the Underboss, who would make a counterproposal. Eventually, if the Boss and Underboss found a common ground, the people who they agreed could drink would drink. Story has it that on more than one occasion, when Sisto was the Boss, if the Underboss didn't see things his way, he just drank all the drinks that had been poured! End of discussion.

Dad loved to tell the story of when one of Aunt Josie's in-laws challenged Sisto to a contest as to who could eat a boiled egg faster. Sisto accepted the bet, two boiled eggs were placed on the table and someone shouted: "Go!" The other gentleman frantically started to crack the egg, anxious to prove how fast he was. Sisto picked up his egg, and placed it in his mouth shell and all, chewed and swallowed. No contest.

It should be clear that Sisto had a temper and his children knew to toe the line. One of Dad's favorite stories about his father was when Dad, at age 10, and his older brother, Joe, at age 12, went down to the Old Mill and stayed out past their curfew of 10 pm. As they walked up Essex Street they could see that Sisto was still awake, sitting at his post at the kitchen window. They knew they were in trouble, for as they walked through the vestibule and down the hall to the apartment door they heard Sisto approaching the door from inside the apartment. They wrestled back and forth as to who would go in the door first, knowing that the first one in was going to get nailed by Sisto. Finally, as the apartment door opened, Sisto grabbed Uncle Joe and gave him a shellacking, as Dad ran past them and hid under one of the beds. But his sanctuary was only to be temporary. After administering his punishment to Uncle Joe, Sisto walked to the bed, balanced himself on one crutch, lifted the bed with his other hand, and using the bed for support, he used his crutch to give Dad his due.

Sisto was not physical with his daughters, but he still ruled with an iron hand. Aunt Angie remembers it as funny now, but wasn't laughing then. As she and Sisto were eating a plate of pasta, he was talking to her but she was not paying attention. After two attempts to get her to listen, he smashed his fist down on the table, saying in broken English: "When I speak 'em, I mean 'em!" His actions caused Aunt Angie's bowl of pasta to completely flip over!

Patience was not a virtue that Sisto possessed. Maybe it was the frustration of having been disabled. Maybe it was trying to raise nine kids during the Depression. Maybe it was just the way he was. Whatever the reason, he was a human Vesuvius, capable of erupting at any moment. Deceptively, to those who didn't

30

know better, he would sit quietly in his favorite chair, with his pipe in his mouth, and his hands intertwined lying peacefully over his stomach – until a trigger event would occur.

One of the most often repeated stories of a Sisto eruption is Aunt Ang's tale of the stuttering radio repairman. Aunt Ang herself stuttered, as did Aunt Carmela and Uncle Louie, so the stage was set for a man like Sisto to get frustrated. One day Aunt Ang was home with her mom, when her mom left to go grocery shopping at the A&P. What Aunt Ang didn't know was that on her way to the store, Grandma stopped by the radio repairman's shop and asked him to come to the house to look at the radio.

Home alone, and more than a bit skittish, Aunt Ang heard a knock at the door, but she wouldn't open it without knowing who was there, and no one responded to her requests for identification. After a few moments, she opened the door to look down the block to see who was there. To her surprise, still standing on the stoop was the radio repairman, holding his repair valise in one hand, beret cocked to one side of his head, and his eyes bulging out of his head as he was still stammering to speak to identify himself.

She let him in and after inspecting and testing the radio, he wanted to tell Aunt Ang his opinion. He tried to say: "Tell your mother, it will be $13.50." That short sentence took him forever: "Tell … Tell … Tell, your mother, your mother, it will be thirteen, thirteen, thirteen." Aunt Ang remembers him sounding like an auctioneer at that point. After finally getting the sentence out, the repairman left.

A week or so later, Aunt Ang came home from school to find both her parents, her sister, Carmela, and the radio repairman in the kitchen. The repairman was stuck on the word "I", repeating it over and over, Aunt Ang not knowing what he was trying to say. Carmela, a teenager at the time, was trying to act as the spokeswoman for the family, and was trying to utter a sentence starting with the word "we" but was having extreme difficulty getting past that one word. Aunt Ang sensing the confusion and hearing a symphony of "I" and "we", tried to tell Carmela "You be quiet" but couldn't do anything but repeat the word "you." Simultaneously, all three were stammering "I ... I ... I" "we ... we ... we" "you ... you ... you." That was the trigger that made Sisto erupt. He yelled out: "Va fungule! Get out! Get out!" and that was the last of the repairman.

Another time Sisto's temper flared was when his sons first tried to help him bathe. Unaware of physics, before trying to lift him out of the tub, they let the water drain out, creating a vacuum, and wedging his big frame in the tub. After he calmed down and had called them some select names, they figured out that if they put water back in the tub, he would float up a little and could be taken out.

Sisto's appetite was legendary, but it was clear that he also had a sense of humor. After polishing off a he-man sized portion of food, and seconds, when asked if he wanted any more to eat, Sisto would respond: "What do you think I am, a horse?" Thanks to Dad's movie films, I have clear pictures in my mind of Sisto enjoying mountains of pizza frita (fried dough), sausages, and other Italian delights.

My dad loved to cook and very often when cooking a meal he would tell us that he was making his dad's recipe. I still make some of those meals today, and I proudly repeat to my children that they are eating Sisto's recipes, food that was once considered "peasant food" but is now all the rage in upscale restaurants. Aunt Ang tells of the time she come home from work and Grandpa Sisto told her to have a seat at the table and he served her a bowl of soup he had made. She liked it and wanted seconds. Sisto insisted that she sit at the table and he would serve her. His insistence that she not get up made her suspicious, and acting on that suspicion she lifted the cover off the pot of soup and saw three sparrows lying in the bottom of the pot, with their feet sticking up through the soup. The following recipes (not including the sparrow soup) were handed down to me from Sisto, through my dad. They are simple dishes, based on vegetables, which was a much less expensive way to feed a family of ten. Each is delicious and every time I make one of them I remind my children, and everyone else at the table, that they are Sisto's recipes.

POP'S STUFFED ARTICHOKES

Dad loved to make stuffed artichokes, and we all loved to eat them. We didn't get them that often as kids, and they were really a treat. Most restaurants now serve them as an appetizer, and charge about $9 or $10 an artichoke! Unbelievable! Mom and Dad used to serve the stuffed artichokes last, after the main meal. We would all sit around and enjoy the artichokes, with after-dinner conversation. As kids we loved the stuffing and Mom loved the heart, which was a little bitter to our tender tastes, so there was always a trade to be made: the leaves from Mom's artichoke, stuffed with breading, for the heart from ours. Like everything else Dad did, he made a competition out of finding the artichoke leaf with the most stuffing. I can still hear him now proclaiming with joy: Look at this one!

4 artichokes, medium to large, not too pointy
2 cups bread crumbs, with Italian seasoning
Parsley
½ cup grated cheese
Olive oil
Salt
Pepper
5-6 cloves of Garlic, diced
Lemon juice
1 ½ cups of hot water
2 cubes chicken bouillon

Pour out a little lemon juice into a small bowl;

Cut the stems off the artichokes, dip cut end of artichoke in lemon juice. Peel stems, cut a slice off the end, and then dice them and place them into the lemon juice;

Cut approximately ¾" off the top of each artichoke, making them flat, and cut off sharp ends of leaves; immediately dip the top of the artichoke into the lemon juice to keep it from turning brown;

In a large bowl, mix approximately two cups of bread crumbs, ½ cup of grated cheese, a sprinkle of Italian seasoning, salt and pepper to taste, a pinch of parsley, and the garlic; stir this mixture and then add enough olive oil to make the mixture moist, but not too wet;

Bang the artichokes onto a cutting board, top side down to open the leaves;

Place the bread crumb mixture generously into the opened leaves and on top of the artichoke;

After the artichokes are stuffed, drizzle with olive oil and sprinkle with grated cheese;

Dissolve two chicken bouillon cubes in 1 ½ cups of hot water; pour chicken bouillon into pot;

Place artichokes into pot and cover. Neither Sisto nor Dad had an electric steam cooker. Luckily I do and it works very well for cooking the artichokes. I use chicken broth instead of water in the bottom well;

Steam for approximately 60 - 70 minutes, depending on size of the artichokes. They are done when leaves can be removed easily.

STUFFED ESCAROLE

The stuffed artichokes I just described, and many variations thereof, can be found in almost every Italian restaurant worth its weight in garlic. But I have not seen Stuffed Escarole anywhere outside of my dad's house, and now mine. He attributed this recipe directly to Sisto.

2 large heads of escarole
1 cup chicken broth

Stuffing: use same stuffing as for Stuffed Artichokes, but add ½ cup of pignolas (pine nuts) and ½ cup of raisins (optional)

Prepare the same stuffing that you would for stuffed artichokes, the only difference is that you will not have the artichoke stems and you will not need the lemon juice. My dad always used pignolas and raisins. I find that some people don't like raisins, and they are optional, but most people like the pignolas.

Wash each of the heads of escarole well; and tie each one loosely with butcher's twine, using a slipknot;

Stuff each head of escarole with the stuffing, being careful not to overstuff them. After they are stuffed, tighten the twine and place the heads of escarole in a large pot, just large enough to contain the two heads, and keep them standing. Add the chicken broth to the bottom of the pot.

Cover, and steam for approximately one half hour.

EGGPLANT SISTO

This is a simple, Old World recipe that can be enjoyed as soon as it is done, and only gets better over a day or two. According to my dad, this is how his father enjoyed eggplant: no breading, no eggs, no tomato sauce, and no mozzarella cheese. As a kid, I wasn't very fond of this, but, boy has it grown on me. You get a much better taste of the eggplant with this dish, and if you are adding fresh basil from your garden, the taste is nothing short of phenomenal.

2 large eggplant, sliced (DO NOT PEEL)
10 cloves garlic, sliced
Olive Oil
Grating Cheese
Basil leaves, cut julienne

Slice the eggplant, horizontally. Place the eggplant in a large colander, sprinkled with salt. Place a plate over the eggplant and weigh it down. My family usually used a large can of tomatoes as a weight. Place the colander over a dinner plate. A small amount of dark liquids will drain from the eggplant. This will reduce any bitterness.

Peel and slice the garlic. Pour enough olive oil into a frying pan so that oil is approximately half an inch thick, and heat. Once the oil is hot, place the garlic in the oil, and fry it until golden brown. With a slotted spoon, remove the garlic and place aside. (The garlic has already served a purpose by infusing its taste into the oil.)

Fry the sliced eggplant until both sides have turned a darker green and the edges brown, but do not burn it. Remove the slices carefully, they will be somewhat mushy, and place them in a glass dish. It's okay to take along a little bit of the olive oil with the eggplant. I usually use a 13″ x 9″ dish. As you finish a layer of eggplant slices, sprinkle them generously with grating cheese, sprinkle some of the fried garlic on top, and sprinkle some of the basil leaves on top. Repeat until you have finished frying all the eggplant.

When this dish is done serve it with a loaf, or two, of Italian bread and watch it disappear. It can be used as an appetizer or as a side dish. It is also outstanding as the condiment on a meat sandwich.

ESCAROLE AND BEANS

This is a great dish for a winter night, but I would not advise having it before being in the company of anyone you are trying to impress. The garlic on your breath would be one drawback, the effect of the beans is quite another. Besides the fantastic taste this dish presents, it is fun pronouncing escarole the Italian way and announcing that you are making "shka-dole." This recipe is also quite versatile. You can omit the pancetta and add several cups of chicken broth and make a delicious wintertime soup, or you can plate the escarole and beans over rice or pasta and make it a main meal. Any way you serve it, it is a very hearty dish that will warm your insides.

2 large heads of escarole
2 tablespoons of olive oil
Salt
Pepper
Crushed red pepper

Rinse the escarole very well, and then chop it up, roughly, or tear it, and then toss it in the olive oil so that it is lightly coated. Place it in a frying pan with a little salt, pepper and crushed red pepper, and cook for approximately ten minutes. Set aside.

2 tablespoons of oil
6 cloves of garlic
4 to 5 ounces of pancetta, diced
Salt
Pepper
Crushed red pepper
2 14 to 16 oz. cans of white
        kidney beans (cannellini), undrained

Heat the olive oil in a frying pan; add the garlic, salt, pepper and crushed red pepper, and pancetta. Cook long enough for the garlic to just start turning color. Do not let the garlic burn or the pancetta get crisp. Add both cans of beans and let that mixture simmer for ten minutes. Then add the cooked escarole, stir together and cook an additional eight to ten minutes.

PASTA FAGIOLI

This is a classic recipe. When we were kids, every Friday night during Lent, when Catholics couldn't eat meat, we would eat eggs scrambled with whatever vegetable was in the house: Potatoes and Eggs, Peppers and Eggs, Squash and Eggs, etc. That was because we had not yet acquired a taste for Pasta Fagioli which was what our parents and grandparents were eating. As we got older, we loved this simple dish, and now my kids look forward to me making it. Since we no longer eat it just on Fridays in Lent, I have expanded the recipe to include bacon and chicken broth for flavor. The original recipe used water instead of broth, and I guess they increased the salt. This recipe is for one pound of pasta; adjust accordingly per pound:

1 medium onion, diced
1 large carrot, diced
2 stalks celery, sliced
2 tablespoons of fat back or bacon
4 cloves of garlic
¼ cup olive oil
Salt, to taste
Pepper, to taste
Crushed red pepper, to taste
Italian seasoning, sprinkle
Parsley, sprinkle
2 cups chicken broth
2 8 oz. cans, or 1 large can tomato sauce (Hunt's or DelMonte)
1 14 – 16 oz. can white kidney beans
1 pound mezza rigatoni, or any other of the smaller pastas which is your
favorite.

Pour olive oil into waterless pot or Dutch oven; heat

Add fat back or bacon and cook for seven to eight minutes;

If you use the fat back, remove it at this time; if you use the bacon you can remove it or leave it in depending on your taste; if you leave it in, break it up;

Add the diced onion, carrot and celery and sauté for approximately four minutes, then add garlic, crushed red pepper, salt, pepper, Italian seasoning and parsley; sauté for an additional three or four minutes;

Add chicken broth, tomato sauce and beans; simmer for an additional ten minutes;

In a separate pot, bring water to boil, and cook pasta al dente;

When pasta is cooked pour it into a strainer and then put pasta into large pot (do not rinse) and add sauce; let it set approximately three or four minutes, serve with generous portions of grated cheese.

When this is freshly made and served, it appears thin and a little soupy (in fact, some restaurants add more liquid and serve it as a soup dish). However, after a while it begins to thicken. And if there are leftovers, when you go to reheat them, it will be quite thick, and may need to be thinned out with a little tomato sauce.

NOTE: Some cooks like to cook the pasta right in the tomato sauce, the starch makes the sauce thicker.

NOTE: Pasta Piselli - If your family does not like beans, or if you would like a pleasant variation, replace beans with one pound of frozen peas. Defrost peas before adding to sauce.

When my dad used peas instead of beans he tended to use small elbows instead of rigatoni. It's a matter of personal taste. Also, with peas, I reduce the amount of hot pepper.

BROCCOLI RABE

Broccoli Rabe is a vegetable that I just didn't appreciate as a kid, but I LOVE now! Actually, although this recipe is included in the chapter on Sisto, I must note I learned through my research that Broccoli Rabe is a plant that is indigenous to the region of Italy known as Basilicata, which includes the town of Pisticci, where my paternal grandmother was born. So this dish may very well have been one of her contributions to the family cookbook.

Broccoli Rabe is really in the turnip family, and is a leafy vegetable that tastes kind of bitter, too bitter, when you are a kid. When your parents wanted you to eat broccoli was bad enough, but this bitter stuff was too much. Funny thing happens when your taste buds mature, though. This vegetable, when sautéed properly with garlic and hot pepper, makes a great basis for pasta and can be complemented with Italian sausage. When my mother's family made this dish they would add pieces of pork or pork kidneys.

3 bunches of Broccoli Rabe
1/3 cup olive oil
5 cloves of garlic
Crushed red pepper, to taste
Salt, to taste
Chicken broth

Take two bowls, one full of cold water and one empty. Rinse the broccoli rabe in the water, one bunch at a time, and place it in the empty bowl after rinsing. After you have rinsed all four bunches, empty out the dirty water and repeat the process until the water is clear after rinsing.

After the broccoli rabe is rinsed, cut off the bottom several inches of the stems, since they are kind of tough. I also remove some of the very large, tough leaves, but be conservative in doing that. The yellow flowers of the vegetable are edible, but most people remove them.

Fill a large pot with salted water; when it comes to a boil, place the broccoli rabe in the pot and blanch, uncovered, for about 5 minutes, until tender. Do not overcook. I hate mushy broccoli rabe.

While the broccoli rabe is being blanched, pour olive oil into waterless pot or Dutch oven; sliver the garlic and add it to the olive oil.

Heat the oil, and after a minute or two add crushed red pepper flakes to the oil and continue to heat, until the garlic turns golden brown.

Remove the broccoli rabe from the water and add it to the oil and garlic, with a dash of salt; toss the broccoli rabe so that it gets a coating of the oil and garlic.

One option is to boil some pasta while you are blanching the broccoli rabe, and add the pasta to the pot for a main course. You can also add pieces of cooked Italian sausage, which makes for a great pasta dish when topped with grated Parmesan or Romano cheese.

Dad with my grandparents, Sisto and Maria, 1943.

Two of my favorite men in the world, Uncle Jimmy "New Haven" (left) and Uncle Sal, my godfather (right).

Neighbors and family in the alleyway of 688 Essex Street. I love this photo because of the young Aunt Angie and Uncle Sal kneeling in front.

Mom and Dad.

CHAPTER 3

THE GREATEST GENERATION

Tom Brokaw christened my mother and father's age group as The Greatest Generation. I am part of what I am sure is the majority of people who grew up idolizing their parents, seeing them as role models when we were youngsters and then gaining a whole new respect for them when we had our own children. I remember feeling that way, and I remember agreeing whole-heartedly with Brokaw when I read his book and marveled at what my parents' generation had endured and accomplished. But as a result of putting together this book and focusing on my parents, my aunts and uncles, and their contemporaries, my admiration for them has reached an all-time high.

It is at this point in writing this book that the first components of what made Brooklyn magical have started to crystallize in my mind. First was the courage shown by the generation that migrated to America and settled in New York. They brought with them their spirit of adventure, their Old World recipes, and their strong sense of family and religion, all of which came to be reflected in the Brooklyn they created. Brooklyn came to be known as The Borough of Churches, with steeples and spires piercing the skyline of homes in every neighborhood in the borough. Restaurants that featured Old World delicacies were within walking distance almost anywhere in the borough. And they weren't just Italian restaurants and pizzerias. There were restaurants featuring the great foods of all the countries the immigrants came from (although almost everybody really thought that the best food was right at home when Mama was in the kitchen).

The next ingredients of Brooklyn's magic were the strength (both mental and physical) and resilience of my parents' generation. The oldest of that generation, like my Uncle Frank, were typically the first children of the immigrants born in America.

They would come to be known as First Generation Americans. They were born to parents who, for the most part, did not speak English, were not yet citizens, and had not yet come close to achieving the American Dream, but for the fact that they were here, which was no small accomplishment in itself. The children who followed were born during World War I, Prohibition, and the Great Depression. As teenagers, or young adults, they saw the World at conflict again and after Japan bombed Pearl Harbor, the young men and women of my parents' generation went to all corners of the World to protect freedom and democracy. Despite suffering the prejudices faced by minority immigrants they effectively integrated into American society and fought for this country, even against the land of their ancestors. Up until the end of World War II, their lives took place against the backdrop of worldwide physical conflict and economic disaster. They knew fear first hand. They learned to live with less by living without. Their greatest asset was family and the company of each other. Despite their terrible life experiences, in Europe and then here, they remained devoted to their families and their religion.

I first marveled at the courage of my grandfather, who as a teenager climbed upon a ship headed to America, not knowing what adventures awaited him. But as my children turned 19 and 20, for the first time I gave real thought to the courage of the young men and women like my father, who was drafted to become a member of the United States Navy before reaching the age of 19, and was sent out on a ship to many ports of call around the world by the age of 20, not with a sense of finding a new life, but probably with a fear of possibly never coming back. He was there at Iwo Jima and Okinawa, as were thousands of others. He was not in the hand to hand combat, yet what he witnessed must have been awfully gruesome, for he never really talked about his years in the Navy during World War II.

As a kid, one of the jobs delegated to me was to write out the envelopes for the Christmas cards my parents sent out. Every year I addressed the envelopes to all of my parents' relatives and friends, most of whom we saw on a regular basis. And every year when I came across the name "Mr. Luke Ocone" I asked my parents who that was, because I never remembered meeting him. My dad told me that Luke was his closest friend in the Navy. They were shipmates on the USS Thurston and toured the South Pacific together. Luke was from New York and he and Dad hit if off really well. It was only when I brought up Mr. Ocone's name that Dad talked about his days in the Navy. So even after I knew who Luke Ocone was I would ask my dad again every year, because it gave him an opportunity to tell me a little bit about their friendship during the war.

While writing this book, eleven years after Dad died, at about Christmas time I remembered Luke Ocone and looked him up on the Internet. It was a fabulous Christmas present when I found his phone number and was able to speak with him. He immediately knew who I was and had great, fond memories of my dad, and their times together in the South Pacific. Mr. Ocone told me that he had indeed met me, when I was about 2 or 3 years old. He knew my whole family, and told me that his dad was the one who crafted the wine press that Sisto, and then my dad, used to make their wine.

Mr. Ocone has provided me with an excellent insight on Dad's naval service. He explained that at Iwo Jima and Okinawa, the Thurston remained close to shore after offloading troops in order to take on wounded military personnel. He explained that he and Dad, and other sailors, worked around the clock to keep the wounded alive until they could deliver them to better medical facilities in Guam. That graphic experience might be why Dad and others didn't talk much about the war experiences. Luke has sent me several photos of him and Dad in the South Pacific, but the stories that he has related have painted a much more telling picture of Dad as a young sailor. It was a special treat when, in 2013, I drove to Luke's home in Pennsylvania, and met him and his wife, Rena.

Dad's naval career started on February 14, 1943 (while he was still 18) with a train ride to Geneva, New York, where he was met by a Chief Petty Officer, and escorted with other recruits to the US Naval Training Center in Sampson, New York. Among Dad's personal effects, which I only found after he passed, was a pamphlet entitled "Helpful Hints for Naval Recruits" which contained the following list of things you should "do" and those you should "not do" which I think should still be distributed to every teenager today:

DO	DO NOT
Pay close attention	Disobey orders or instructions
Carry out orders	Borrow money or effects
Keep your clothes marked	Lend money or effects
Keep your effects neat	Buy on credit (always pay cash)
Select good friends	Leave anything adrift
Write home regularly	Hitch hike
Be proud of the Navy	Be friendly with strangers who promise
Be courteous to visitors	you a good time
Learn your general orders	Try to be funny on duty
Take a shower daily	Wear another man's clothes or sleep
Take care of your feet	in his hammock
Save your money	Use another man's drinking cup, tooth
Report subversive talk	brush or towel

After boot camp Dad trained at Camp Allen, Naval Operations Base in Norfolk, Virginia. That is where, as a Pharmacist's Mate Second Class (PhM 2/C) he first learned about taking x-rays, which became his livelihood as a civilian. Ultimately, he was assigned to the USS Thurston (77), known affectionately as The Mighty T. Mr. Ocone told me that he and Dad earned spending money by developing their fellow sailors' photos in the x-ray dark room. He also told me that among the "medical supplies" were bottles of whiskey, and they would dispense one ounce at a time to injured sailors, as a primitive pain-killer, I guess. If a sailor declined they would note that he took the whiskey and when 32 ounces was unused but accounted for, he and Dad would trade a full bottle with the ship's cook in exchange for steak or pork chops.

The Thurston left Norfolk, Virginia on December 21, 1944, with Dad (and Luke) aboard, headed for the Pacific. Dad crossed the Panama Canal for the first time on December 27, 1944. Once through the Panama Canal, the Thurston continued on to San Francisco arriving on January 5, 1945. I remember Dad telling me that as the ship headed towards California around Christmastime, the sailors were singing "I'm dreaming of a white mistress." He liked to tell the story that while in San Francisco, he ate Fried Calamari at a restaurant called Sabella's at Fisherman's Wharf, and when I visited San Francisco in 2007, I made sure that I visited Sabella's, sat at the same counter Dad did in 1945, and I ordered Fried Calamari in his honor. He also said that while at Fisherman's Wharf, with Luke, they were sitting in a restaurant and noticed that Joe DiMaggio, a San Francisco native who strongly guarded his privacy, was sitting at a corner table. Fearing that he had been identified, DiMaggio turned off the lamp at his table and quietly sat in the dark to remain unnoticed to others.

After boarding troops in San Francisco, the Thurston headed for Hawaii, and arrived there, at Pearl Harbor, on January 22, 1945. After exchanging troops the Thurston headed to the Marianas, via Eniwetok in the Marshall Islands. In fact, the Thurston's real mission was to bring troops to Iwo Jima. From February 11 to February 16 she was at Saipan, where she sortied with Transport Group Able of the Attack Force for the assault against the Japanese island of Iwo Jima.

Reports from sailors on the USS Thurston relate that after leaving Hawaii the ship received a radio message from Tokyo, actually from Tokyo Rose to be exact. She said, "This is Tokyo Rose. I'm speaking primarily to the crew and officers of the Mighty T., the U.S.S Thurston. We know where you are, and you are not going to reach your destination." That verbal assault was

53

followed by two submarine attacks but the Thurston, and my dad, avoided any damage.

Dad, and the Thurston, reached Iwo Jima on February 19, 1945, the beginning of the attack on Iwo Jima, entitled Operation Detachment, and remained off the beaches of Iwo Jima until February 26. It was during that time, five days into the operation, that the legendary raising of the American flag by the US Marines at Mt. Suribachi was photographed, and that was one thing Dad did talk about, seeing that flag being raised. The sailors on board the ship had heard a rumor that the Marines were about to raise a flag on Mt. Surabachi so most of them rushed up to the deck. The ship was too far from the site so Dad and Luke watched Mt. Surabachi through the telescopic sights of one of the deck guns, which were not manned at the time. While they waited and watched they were eating dry bologna sandwiches carried by mess cooks to the crew in huge aluminum dishpans. When the flag went up all the sailors on the ship celebrated, accepting the gesture as a sign of victory, meaning the Thurston could soon leave this arena of war. Iwo Jima was one of the fiercest battles of the Pacific, lasting until March 26, 1945. It is estimated that the United States lost 6,825 of its troops on that island, while the Japanese suffered almost 18,000 casualties. From Iwo Jima, the Thurston travelled toward the Marianas and arrived back at Saipan on March 2, then on to Guam, and then to Tulagi in the Solomon Islands and Espiritu Santo.

In the early 1940s the lines of communication between those in service and their loved ones back home were limited to mail and telegrams. The soldiers and sailors who were not actively in combat might also have access to a phone, but the cost of long distance phone service and the limited availability made it virtually a non-factor even for them. Without texting, instant messaging, or the Internet, the mail was really their only means to stay in touch; but long before our generation came up with email, the generation before us had V• • • ■ Mail. (The symbol configuration between the V and Mail, three dots and a dash, is Morse Code for V, with the V standing for Victory.)

Modeled after Great Britain's Airgraph service, the United States Post Office Department developed V● ● ● ▬ Mail as early as 1938 as an emergency mail service in anticipation of the problems that would be encountered during wartime, problems created by the sheer volume of those wanting to communicate with their loved ones compounded by the logistics of war. There was also a concern that space on vessels would be limited and necessary to transport war supplies and could not be dedicated to mail. The system that was devised integrated microfilm technology. V● ● ● ▬ Mail forms were available to civilians in the States and were made available to members of the military. The sender would write their message on the form, address it, and then fold, seal and deposit the form in a mail box. Members of the military could send the form free of postage. The forms were passed through military censors who blacked out military secrets or sensitive materials. The letters were then copied onto microfilm, which was shipped overseas, saving shipping space. When the microfilm arrived at its destination it was reproduced at one quarter of the original size at a processing station, and it was then delivered to the addressee.

My dad's oldest sister, Josephine, (who we all called Aunt Josie), saved some of Dad's letters home during his Navy days. Thanks to her daughter, my cousin, Antoinette, who was gracious enough to give me copies of those letters, I have been given a glimpse of that time. As I read the letters, I could feel my dad's love for his family coming through, together with his sense of humor and his desire to be back home. The first letter I have is dated March 19, 1945. At that time the Thurston was at sea. Interestingly, although it was only three weeks after Dad's experiences at Iwo Jima, he never mentioned either the invasion or the raising of the flag. He also didn't mention that he was headed to Okinawa. It could be that he didn't know where he was headed, or he knew where he was going and didn't say, because all of the mail had to be reviewed by the Naval Censor first, (as indicated by the seal on all envelopes from Dad), to remove any facts which would endanger security, or he didn't want the family to worry about him.

Dear Sis,

I just received a couple of your letters that were dated away back, some letters get through very fast & some very slow, at any rate it was swell hearing from you. I'll bet you must have your hands full right now with Antoinette, Marie & Mickey with the whooping cough, how are they getting along?

I just finished writing Antoinette a letter & told her about the beer party we had today. I only had a couple of bottles of beer. I spent most of my time playing baseball. We swam with the tropical fish. We tried to catch them but they were much too fast. *** Also tried to go into the jungle but it was too dense. It was so thick you couldn't see five foot ahead. I must have seen a million palm trees. I ate so many coconuts, it wouldn't bother me a bit not to see one again.

I hear Jerry doesn't like working for the Army, he doesn't know how lucky he is. I'd even shovel snow to be back home.

We went fishing over the side of the ship, everybody caught at least one fish but me. All I got back was the hook without the bait, it was gone four times. I'll just have to catch a fish before this cruise is up, or I'll lose a lot of prestige.

I'll say so long now & regards to all.

Jim

When I shared this letter with Luke Ocone, he told me that another thing Dad left out of the letter, not wanting to worry his family, was that while he was in the jungle, with Luke, they were fired upon. They were in the Philippines, in the Sibuyan

Sea, on shore for a recreational break. Luke and Dad walked into the jungle, which they had been warned was forbidden. According to Luke: "It was hot, very humid, lush with vines and other vegetation and the air was filled with insects. However, we were curious and kept walking, and eventually we came upon a group of huts. Amidst these huts there was a pyramidal structure consisting of shelves, and seated on the bottom shelf there were two very old-looking women smoking cigars and playing cards with a strange, colorful deck. They may have been members of a militant Muslim minority called Moros. They paid little attention to us, and after a few minutes, we kept walking into the jungle. Suddenly, we heard gunshots and the sound of bullets ripping through the foliage around us. Both of us crouched as low as we could and ran as fast as we could in that uncomfortable position."

Less than two weeks later, on April 9, 1945, the Thurston came into port at Hagushi Beach on Okinawa, right smack dab in the middle of Operation Iceberg, the US invasion of Okinawa. Although the Thurston was a troop transport and not a battleship or destroyer, she was not out of harm's way. When the ship was fully loaded with troops she was a worthy target of a number of kamikaze pilots, especially since it was basically a lightly armed cargo vessel. Luckily, and against the odds, she escaped damage. The battle of Okinawa has been called the Typhoon of Steel referring to the huge number of American and Allied ships and armored vehicles and the constant barrage of kamikaze suicide attacks they endured. It is estimated that by the time the battle ended in June 1945, 12,500 Allied troops had been killed with an additional 38,000 wounded, while 95,000 Japanese had been killed and 7,000 to 10,000 captured.

After leaving Okinawa the Thurston continued to transport troops around the South Pacific, on the very days during the first week of August 1945, that the United States dropped atomic bombs on Hiroshima and Nagasaki in Japan. The Thurston finally anchored in San Francisco on August 14, 1945, which was VJ Day, (Victory over Japan), Japan having surrendered that day.

The Thurston was one of the first war ships to pass under the Golden Gate Bridge on VJ Day and Dad and Luke had "liberty" that night. San Francisco celebrated the victory over Japan with the worst riots in the city's history. Dad and Luke ducked into a bar and nursed a few drinks until the craziness subsided.

With all of the Axis powers having surrendered, the ship's sailors' activities, and Dad's letters, portrayed a sense of relief. I remember him showing me pictures of himself and his fellow sailors cutting up as part of a ritual known as Crossing the Line, when all those sailors who had never before crossed the Equator, known as Pollywogs, were initiated by their more experienced shipmates, when summoned to appear before the Court of Neptune, a mock tribunal comprised of the veteran sailors. He was still in the Navy on November 13, 1945, when, on stationery bearing the inscription U.S.S. Thurston (AP77) he wrote:

Dearest Josie & Jerry,

I received a V-mail from you yesterday & it was swell hearing that all is fine at home.

It's been raining all day today & all I did was address Christmas cards. I'll mail them about December 1 or so. They should get there by Christmas.

I had to laugh at Mickey eating 5 frankfurters. I wonder who he takes after, surely it couldn't be me, as five hot dogs was only an appetizer to me.

So you're saving some whiskey for me. I wonder what kind it is, it should be aged & mellow by the time I get home. Seriously, I should be a civilian surely by April, the same with Joe or even sooner with him.

You asked if we celebrated Navy Day. On Navy Day we were bouncing around in a storm & had no time to celebrate.

Joe must be having a swell time in China, according to his letters anyway. I wonder if he's being true to Connie. I wish I was in China. I'd get about ten Chinese wives & live like a King.

I must have dish pan hands, all I got was two dates in Seattle, two nice girls, darn it! I like naughty girls. So long & loads of love to the "3."

Jim

On February 6, 1946, while aboard the USS Thurston in the South Pacific, after having received a V● ● ● ▬ Mail from Aunt Josie and Uncle Jerry, Dad wrote:

Dear Josie & Jerry,

I received your V-mail dated Jan. 31 & I was very glad to hear from you.

I guess you heard about the news of us going to China or haven't you heard yet? Yep, we leave 2-15-46, & we're due back the first week in April & that's when I'll be discharged.

***

So you don't think I'll enjoy myself when I get to be a civilian. Well, that's yet to be seen at any rate, it can't be worse than being in the Navy!

***

I'll bet you're glad Joe is out, that's one letter less you have to write. I wonder how many letters I wrote since I've been in.

So long & regards to all!

Jim

The "Joe" that Dad was referring to was his brother who was in the Army the same time that Dad was in the Navy, both of them overseas.

In the 1600s, John Milton wrote "They also serve who stand and wait." It was the last line in one of his poems, written to declare that despite the disability he had, blindness, he had a place and purpose in this life, as we all do. That line of poetry could have been written three hundred years later, to describe the service performed by the wives, mothers, and other family members of those who were in active military service around the world during World War II. Aunt Josie was a lover of poetry who could recite some of the great poems of history verbatim. I especially remember her passionate recital of Walt Whitman's "O Captain! My Captain!" at family parties. Actually, recital is too weak a word. She performed that poem, making you feel the love the poet had for Lincoln, and his enormous grief suffered at the loss of his "Captain." Her early love for poetry and her feelings for her family are clear in a poem of her own, written while her brothers were overseas. It captures the feelings of many others waiting at home for their loved ones to return:

Brothers of Mine

Oh how I miss those brothers of mine,
They're gone for such a long long time.
It's only months but it seems like years
Each night I lie awake in tears.

I miss their teasing and all our fights
I yearn for the pillows that flew of nights,
I miss them whenever I feel like dancing
I miss my watching his cute romancing.

He'd pinch my cheeks and he'd pinch my nose
Until they'd look like a red, red rose
They'd throw the soap and I'd fling the pie
And we'd laugh until we thought we'd die

But they'll come back and we'll have lots more
Of fighting over who goes to the store

I remember my Aunt Angie, the youngest of my dad's siblings, always telling me some of her memories as a young girl with several brothers serving at once. Two memories stand out, one a little funny and the other an emotional reminder of the anxiety that families experienced while their loved ones defended freedom around the world.

First the humorous: Thanksgiving, as you can imagine and will come to read later in this book, was a big holiday in the Sabellico household, as it was, and is, in most homes in America. But when my father was in the Navy there was no way that his mother was going to allow a celebration to occur at home. She wanted her boys home safe and sound, and when that happened then there would be a celebration. So, Aunt Angie relates that as Thanksgiving approached in 1943 she asked her mother why no holiday preparations were happening, and she was told that they would not be celebrating while brother Jim was not home, and they had a simple meal that Thanksgiving. A few weeks later they received mail from my Dad, which included a copy of the holiday menu he was served by the Navy, including Roast Turkey with Giblet Gravy, Whipped Potatoes, Mashed Turnips, String Beans, Cranberry Sauce, Mince Pie, Nesselrode Pudding, Apples and Tangerines. Aunt Angie remembers reading about what a feast the Navy served, (at least it all sounded good on paper), while they did without at home. They all had a good laugh about it, which they needed. They all missed Dad much more than a fancy meal, and they prayed for his safe return when they could all feast together.

Aunt Ang's second recollection is much more poignant. The one thing that families with children at war dreaded was a telegram. It almost always meant news that a loved one had died in service to America. Aunt Ang has shared this story with me several times, through fresh tears of agony every time (although the event happened seventy years ago): in July 1944, Aunt Ang was at home with her mother when the doorbell rang and when asked to identify himself the visitor announced that he had a telegram for Mrs. Sabellico. Hearing the word "telegram" my grandmother immediately began to cry and wail; she pulled at her hair and at her clothing, sure that she was about to receive news that one of her sons died in service. Aunt Ang, just 11 years old at the time, cried at the sight of her mother's torment and didn't know what to do. The messenger calmed everyone down long enough to explain to my aunt that the telegram was from my Uncle Joe who was in the service overseas, and its message was simply "Happy Birthday Mom."

Just recently I evidenced the continuing impact of war on my parents' generation. While talking to Aunt Angie about the fact that several of her brothers served in World War II, and her youngest brother, my Uncle Sal, lied about his age to enlist in the Navy, she recited, without error, through tears, Robert Service's poem, *Young Fellow My Lad*, the first stanza of which is as follows:

"Where are you going, Young Fellow My Lad,
On this glittering morn of May?"
"I'm going to join the Colours, Dad;
They're looking for men, they say."
"But you're only a boy, Young Fellow My Lad;
You aren't obliged to go."
"I'm seventeen and a quarter, Dad,
And ever so strong, you know

My mom's life before meeting my dad was not quite as whirlwind, yet it also tells a story about her and her generation. She attended Wadleigh High School in Manhattan, and by reading her high school yearbook I learned that she was an excellent student. Her yearbook recited that she was an honor student and a member of the Arista Society. Arista was the forerunner of the National Honor Society. Scholarship, service and character were the characteristics that faculty advisors were to look for in nominating students to the Arista Society. As I got older I could verify her intelligence and her work ethic from first-hand experience. I got to work in the same law office with my mom, and I can attest to the fact that scholarship, service and character were three traits of her professional life which were not only present but outstanding. In her personal life, it would be her love for and devotion to her family.

When she was sixteen years old Mom went to work for her cousin, Ralph Cavallo, who was an attorney. Also working in that office as attorneys were Maurice Sutta, Nathan Frankel, and Frank Reiter, men who Mom would go on to work for as a legal secretary for over 37 years, and who I would come to know and respect as uncles. While Dad was off fighting World War II, Mom was starting her career as a legal secretary. When you compare what employees earn today, and the benefits they are provided with, you learn a lot about the character of Mom's generation from the following: she started out earning about $5 a week, and when fall turned to winter her employers realizing she did not have a winter coat, sent her over to Gimbels on 32nd Street and 6th Avenue, and lent her the money to buy a cloth coat. They then deducted 50 cents a week from her pay until they were repaid.

When World War II was over, veterans like my dad, at the age of 22, came back to the States and helped build a modern America. They were the generation who built skyscrapers as well as thousands of one-family homes that defined suburbia. They built the Interstate Highway System creating a sophisticated traffic grid allowing convenient cross-country travel, and simultaneously they were the driving force behind landing an American on the moon. Their research was the basis for landmark breakthroughs in science and communications.

Yet, all of those monumental accomplishments aside, maybe the greatest attribute of the members of my parents' generation was their ability to make something from very little, to accomplish against all odds, and to live within their means as they created what they thought was a better life for their children. Here's an insight as to the magic of the time of my childhood in Brooklyn: almost everything we take for granted now, and all of the comforts of life that our children think come standard with life, were not part of everyday life for members of my parents' generation. Some of them were just starting to appear back in the late 1950s and early 1960s. For the generation that had endured the Depression and World War II, it was magic to see telephones and televisions in every house. And just around 1960, Princess phones, touch tone dialing, and color television were breaking on the scene. Automobiles were becoming more readily available to the middle class, and they were starting to look great. Who among us has not been awed by the look of a '57 Chevy, still today? Imagine how they felt about them then. Appliances that made housewives' lives more bearable were being introduced, although we didn't own most of them, including a dishwasher or a clothes dryer. How much better could life be?

And a complementary factor of the magic of that time was that many of the conveniences present today did not exist at all back then: video recorders, digital cameras, fax machines, videos, DVDs, Internet, computers, video games. No, the members of The Greatest Generation had not yet invented all of that for us; we, and they, just had each other, simply, and we enjoyed it. Without texting and Instant Messaging, we just had to wait until tomorrow to talk to our best friends. Without VCRs and TiVo, we watched a show, or sporting event, if Mom and Dad were not using the family TV, and if they allowed us, or we missed it and waited until tomorrow to read about it in the New York Daily News. Without digital cameras, our parents took pictures, or we did, with our Kodak Brownie or Instamatic, and we sent the film away to be developed. Two or three weeks later, it was another event when the mailman delivered our photos. Without video cameras or camcorders as they came to be known, we were left to the world of silent 8 mm films, which also took a few weeks to be developed. We would use our imagination and our memory to fill in the sounds of the moments our parents had recorded.

I need to share with you how rich those moments were. Of the dozens of reels of 8 mm films that my dad took, there are two, both taken before I was born, which stand out in my mind that help to describe the generations that went before me in creating the magic of my time in Brooklyn.

The first is a film my dad took on New Year's Eve. The party was held in my parents' apartment and it appears that the whole Sabellico family was there. The film is silent only in the technical sense, for your mind convinces you that you can hear the youthful giggling of my older cousins as kids and you can sense the jingling of coins as the family plays a card game called Seven and a Half. When the scene shifts to a view of the ham being basted in the oven, your mouth waters anticipating its sweetness, accompanied by the cherries, pineapple, cloves, and brown sugar that make it a Virginia Ham. But richest is the scene at midnight. As the camera shows the clock nearing 12 midnight you see my aunts and uncles equipping themselves with pots and pans, and spoons and cans of food – the precursors to today's noisemakers, and when the camera catches the clock with both hands straight up, Dad pans the room to catch the traditional exchange of kisses and hugs among all members of the family. It is a very poignant clip of film which follows my grandmother, with streaming tears of happiness, trying to make her way through the crowd to Sisto, who is seated on the other side of the room. Every foot along the way she receives another kiss and hug, which she absorbs lovingly, while never taking her eye off her husband, the target of her trip across the room and her love. When she gets there, their embrace is worth it all! Neither Hepburn and Tracy nor Rogers and Astaire did it any better!

The other classic was the first film Dad ever recorded and it was done over a two day period. It was taken in 1949, on the night before Thanksgiving and on Thanksgiving Day in his parents' home. During the course of that twenty minute film, you see my dad's parents making homemade sausage and stuffing two turkeys as they prepared a feast for their family. While they were preparing the food, the scene kept shifting to the front door, as each of my dad's siblings, together with his or her spouse and kids came in. A special moment was Uncle Sal entering the kitchen wearing his Navy uniform, home on leave for Thanksgiving. Every face was filled with love and happiness to be there. There were no exquisite outfits, no magnificent jewelry, no large gifts or floral sprays. Just my aunts, uncles and cousins, all happy to be at Grandma and Grandpa's. Again, though the film was silent, I can hear their voices and their laughs, I can feel their embraces.

As the scene shifts to the Thanksgiving table, one is amazed at the fullness of the feast. The French doors which separated the living room and the master bedroom were swung open, and the furniture pushed aside to make room for a table that spanned two rooms. Every single member of the family was there. In your mind, you can hear Sisto laughing as he poured another glass of red wine from the gallon. Uncle Sal's smile is so bright it seems to burn a hole in the screen. You can hear Uncle Jerry laughing as he pumped up the pressure on the half keg of beer the family had in the kitchen for the Thanksgiving dinner. Aunt Angie's youthful glamour catches your breath. Then you witness a family ritual which would be unheard of today. They passed around the turkey drumstick, and every member of the family took a bite of it. And everyone did it. No one wiped their mouth or the drumstick. No one looked for a "clean" part to bite. They were all family, and as you watch the drumstick make its way around the table you can feel the juice of the meat run down your chin and you just so wish you were sitting at that table.

That film from Thanksgiving of 1949 starts with Sisto and Maria taking a mountain of ground pork and stuffing it into casings, making sausages for the Thanksgiving holiday. The following recipes are presented together to give you an idea of the mindset of that time. Nothing went to waste. If you were going to make Italian Sausage, you bought a pork shoulder butt. After you removed the skin (which was saved to make a delicious braciole), you then trimmed a good deal of the fat off of the pork before cutting up the rest to feed into the grinder. The meat was used for the sausage, but the fat (lard) was used to make delicious bread.

Another recipe I have added allows you total creativity in the kitchen. This recipe started out as Italian Vegetable Stew which was a staple especially during the summer, using homegrown vegetables. It is called Giambatta, and came to be pronounced "jom-bort" which became a euphemism for making a stew-like dish from whatever you had lying around in the kitchen. I am positive that if you speak with any Italian-American of my generation and you mention Giambatta, they will laugh and shake their head at the memory of the mixture, how it was different every time you had it, and how unbelievable it is that you have the same memories that they do.

Also indicative of how my parents' generation made do with what they had, Uncle Sal would tell me that many mornings the breakfast he and his siblings enjoyed was day old Italian bread, soaked in black coffee (espresso) and sprinkled with sugar. That might not be a breakfast recommended by the United States Department of Agriculture in their "food pyramid" but it was an effective use of yesterday's leftovers, helped feed a family of eleven, and provided memories that we are still talking about seventy years later. Aunt Ang remembers that on many a winter morning before she, Uncle Sal and Aunt Antoinette went off to school, her mother gave her a beverage which consisted of a raw egg, sugar, milk and a shot of whiskey!

The recipes I am including aren't the important thing. They are merely symbolic of the thinking of the family and thousands of others like it in Brooklyn. They made the most of what they had. They cherished each other and their existence here in America. They focused on what they had, not on what they were lacking. There was no telling them they were poor, not with a roof over their heads, wine in the cellar, a yard full of fire wood and home-grown vegetables, and a house full of children, grandchildren and love for each other.

Just another quick story to make my point before we get to the recipes. After the older children were all married, and Grandma Maria had passed away, Aunt Ang, still only in her early twenties, continued to live at home with Grandpa Sisto. One Sunday morning she took a pound of chopped meat and began to add the ingredients to make meatballs for her and Sisto. The phone rang with the news that one of her brothers would be coming over with his family for dinner. She added additional breadcrumbs and cheese to the mix to stretch it out. Fifteen minutes later she received another call, and then another. By the time she finished adding breadcrumbs and other ingredients, Aunt Ang had stretched that meat out to make twenty-eight meatballs! They may not have tasted as good or rich as originally intended, but you know what? They were all eaten, the family all ate together, and the story of how Aunt Ang made do that Sunday morning has been told and re-told to the extent that it has become the Sabellico equivalent of the time Jesus fed the multitudes with a limited number of loaves and fishes.

ITALIAN SAUSAGE

10 pounds ground pork shoulder butt, cut and ground
10 tsp salt
2 tbp coarse black pepper
1 tbsp cracked fennel seed (optional)
Paprika (optional)
Red pepper flakes (optional)
Garlic (optional)
Parsley (optional)
Casings

Prepare the casings the day before by soaking in water with a pinch of salt.

Cut the meat off the bone, into cubes about 2 inches in size, keeping the fat but not any sinew.

Grind the meat and keep it cold until you are ready to add seasonings.

Combine all seasoning and mix well into ground pork, using your hands. I suggest that before you stuff the sausage mixture into the casings you take a few tablespoons of it and fry it in a little water. Then you can adjust the seasonings to your taste so your sausage comes out perfect.

When you are happy with the seasoned meat, tie one end of the casing and attach the other end to stuffing machine. Then stuff into casings; try to limit the amount of air that gets into casings.

When finished, tie off the end of the casing. Then tie off the sausage into links of about 4 inches, and prick the sausage links with a sharp object (knife, pin, etc.) to release any trapped air.

Keep in mind there are a few keys to making successful sausages for your family:

1. The meat cannot be too lean, nor too fat. You want about 80% lean meat and about 20% meat which has fat content. If the meat is too lean the sausage will be dry and tasteless; if the meat is too fat the sausage will be oily;

2. You need to adjust the seasonings to your family's tastes, using the above recipe as a starting point, not an end. Some people like fennel, some prefer caraway seeds. Some people like to add Italian Seasoning, or parsley, or cheese and basil. Some people like to add hot pepper flakes. I have heard that some people add a little red wine. Just as people have gotten creative with pizzas, sausage is no longer just "sweet" or "hot." There are many varieties, including adding vegetables, like broccoli rabe, or changing the meat mixture, to add beef, or just using chicken or turkey. Have fun with it. Use trial and error and adjust it to your family's tastes.

LARD BREAD

Aunt Ang told me that when her mom and dad made lard bread, it was too big to fit in the oven in the kitchen. So her brothers would place the uncooked bread on a board and put it on top of the baby carriage, and she and Aunt Jean would take the bread to the bakery, where the baker would cook it for 25 cents!

1 lb. pork, cut in small pieces, from a picnic or butt
Grating cheese
Raisins
Pignola
1 pizza dough (see Pizza Dough Recipe)

If you don't have time to make the pizza dough, you can cheat a little and purchase it from a local pizzeria. Purchase one ball of dough (what they use to make one pizza) for each bread you intend to make.

Ingredients should never be placed on the dough while they are hot. So it is important to cook and cool all ingredients in advance of making the bread.

Trim approximately one pound of meat and fat, not skin, from a pork butt or picnic. Cut the pieces in cubes, approximately 1". Place the meat and fat in a frying pan with a very small amount of oil. Cook the meat down until golden brown. Remove the solid pieces from the oil with a slotted spoon and place aside. Pour the liquid from the frying pan into a bowl and place in the refrigerator. This step must be completed several hours before you intend to bake the bread. The liquid will solidify into lard in the refrigerator.

Preheat oven to 325 degrees.

Stretch the dough and spread it out on the tabletop until it has the appearance of a shape of a pizza – about 16" across.

Scoop out a small amount of the lard with your fingertips and spread it over the dough, so that all the dough is coated with a very thin layer of the lard. Sprinkle the fried pieces of meat and pork fat over the dough; then place raisins, to your taste, and pignola, to your taste over the dough; then sprinkle with grated cheese and black pepper.

Roll the dough, like a jellyroll, until the seam is on the bottom, then coil the dough, like a coffee roll. Place the roll onto an ungreased cookie sheet.

Using your fingers take another small portion of the lard and apply a thin layer to the outside of the bread, then sprinkle with grated cheese and black pepper.

Bake at 325 – 350 degrees for 35 to 40 minutes, depending on your oven.

Let bread set at least 20 minutes before eating. THIS BREAD IS BEST EATEN VERY WARM, AND PART OF THE FUN IS RIPPING IT APART, NOT CUTTING IT.

It was customary to eat this bread on Christmas Eve, after midnight. Only fish and seafood were served during the Christmas Eve vigil, but not content with that, Italian families would prepare another meal to eat after midnight. Usually we made our own sausage and the meat for the sausage came from the pork butt or picnic. In trimming the butt or picnic, we were left with the fat and pieces, which would not go to waste. They formed the basis for the lard bread. Enjoy!

PIGSKIN BRACCIOLE

3 pieces pig skin, long enough to roll about 3 times, about 8" square
Equal amounts (about a handful) of:

Grated cheese
Parsley
Raisins
Pignola
Breadcrumbs

Salt and pepper to taste
Butcher's twine

Rinse skins in warm water, rinse and pat dry. Lay skins out on the table, making sure that the rind side is down. Mix all other ingredients, making sure not to use too much salt if you are using sharp grating cheese, and sprinkle a generous amount on each skin. Roll skins and tie with twine, making sure to tie around each skin and to tie string from end to end. End by tying the string in a knot.

Sauté the bracciole in oil until lightly browned, but not crisp. Place the browned bracciole in your tomato sauce, and make sure they get to cook in the sauce for at least an hour. Remove with the rest of the meat, cut and remove all string, slice the bracciole and top with a little of the tomato sauce.

I believe that this dish is Sicilian in origin. I don't know how it got into my family repertoire, but I guess it came from one of my Sicilian aunts: Aunt Jean, Aunt Nellie, or Aunt Connie. Whoever it was – thanks!

PIZZA DOUGH

1 (.25 ounce) package active dry yeast
2 cups warm water
2 tablespoons olive oil
1 teaspoon salt
1 tablespoon sugar
6 cups flour

In a 4 cup measuring cup, or small bowl holding at least three cups, combine warm water, yeast, olive oil, salt and sugar, stir lightly. Let stand until yeast starts to bubble, approximately five minutes.

Place flour in large mixing bowl. Add yeast mixture into mixing bowl with flour.

Combine all of the ingredients. Don't be afraid to use your hands. Then mix with electric mixer, using dough hooks, until dough forms.

Remove dough from mixing bowl, shape into a ball and place in a clean large bowl. Cover, with a damp cloth, and let sit (and rise) for 3 to 5 hours, until the dough has approximately doubled in volume.

When the dough has doubled, pinch it down to eliminate air bubbles, and then the dough is ready to be stretched out and used.

GIAMBATTA

You would have to try to make this recipe wrong. The list of ingredients is merely a suggestion. The amount of the ingredients is also a suggestion. Maybe you like eggplants more than zucchini. Maybe you don't like mushrooms. Maybe you have a few extra peppers that will go bad if you don't use them. That is the kind of dish this is. It allows you to use whatever is coming out of the garden or whatever is leftover in the kitchen. Feel creative? Look around the kitchen and get cooking. This dish was served very often in the summer and was very helpful I feeding a large family. Serve it over rice, pasta or crusty Italian bread and you can't go wrong.

¼ cup olive oil
1 large onion, diced
2 lbs. Italian sausage, hot or sweet, or other meat (optional)
2 or 3 bell peppers, red or green, chopped
2 or 3 large tomatoes, chopped
(or use 1 28 oz. can of diced or crushed tomatoes)
2 or 3 potatoes, diced
3 or 4 cloves of garlic, diced
2 carrots, diced
1 medium eggplant, diced
½ lb. mushrooms, sliced
2 or 3 zucchini, diced or sliced
½ lb. green beans, cut and blanched
Salt and pepper, to taste
6 or 7 leaves of basil, torn in pieces

Place oil and onion in a large Dutch oven, salt and pepper to taste. Add sausage if desired, and cook until onions are translucent and sausage is browned.

Add such other vegetables as you desire, in the order of adding those which take the longest to cook first. Stir all ingredients and place cover on Dutch oven. Cook for approximately 25 minutes with cover on; then remove cover, stir and continue to cook for approximately 15 to 20 minutes on medium heat.

Sabellico family at Uncle Lou and Aunt Millie's Wedding, April 1940. Standing, left to right: Aunt Carmela, Uncle Lou, Uncle Joe, Dad, Grandpa Maria, Uncle Frank, Uncle Sal, Aunt Josie; Seated: left to right: Aunt Angie, Grandpa Sisto, Aunt Antoinette.

My seven oldest cousins in front of 688 Essex Street: Marie Santangelo, Mickey Santangelo, Marie Sabellico, Frank Sabellico, Libby Sabellico, Anthony Sabellico, Antoinette Santangelo.

Dad swinging a bat, January 1943.

Me swinging a bat, April 1958.

Dad (second from right) walking off Dexter Park field with Franklin K. Lane High School team.

CHAPTER 4

BASEBALL

If you know me, you know I am a baseball fanatic. I love the game. I loved playing it as a kid. I love coaching it. I love watching it and discussing it. Although there are so many sports available for kids to play, follow and pursue now, I believe that baseball will always hold a special place for many of us because at its simplest core it is a game of catch, one of the first games we learned as toddlers, as our parents rolled us a ball and we rolled it back. Well, for me, it was a little more intense than that.

Dad always loved baseball, and his brother Joe, the closest to him in age, was his most frequent playmate and teammate. Uncle Frank was 13 years older than Dad and so many responsibilities had been foisted on him that baseball was not a luxury afforded to him. Uncle Louie was not into baseball; boxing was his thing. I don't think he was too good at it though. I remember him telling me that as a boxer he had to have surgery once to have the canvas removed from his back. (He was the joker among the brothers.) And Uncle Sal was too young to play when Uncle Joe and Dad were in their heyday. But I do remember that whenever the subject of baseball came up Uncle Sal would proudly tell the story of how he hit a ball from the backyard of 688 Essex Street to the lawn of the Pride of Judea Orphanage on Linwood Street on the other side of New Lots Avenue! That shot, and that story, were his baseball moments of glory. It must have been tough to get any notice when you were the youngest of five brothers.

Aunt Ang relates how Uncle Sal idolized my dad, and has told me of an incident that bore out their love for each other. Dad and Uncle Joe were playing on the same team, on the fields between Fountain Avenue and Euclid Avenue, just north of Linden Boulevard and Uncle Sal was there cheering. In the bottom of the ninth inning, Dad hit a home run to win the game. Uncle Sal was razzing the other team, bragging about his brother, when their boiling point was reached and they started to go after him. Dad jumped over the bench and ran across the field to defend his brother and restored peace.

Dad loved to tell the story of Otto, the Swedish handyman, who spoke with a thick accent. It appears that Dad and Uncle Joe, while playing baseball, caused the ball to go through one of the windows at 688 Essex Street. Sisto called on Otto to replace the window pane, which back then required a piece of glass to be cut to size, and placed in the frame with putty and secured by nailing in a thin molding using brads. As Otto was just about completing the job, and was about to hammer in the brads, my dad warned him, "Be careful you don't break the window" to which Otto replied: "You think my name is Yimmy or Yoey?"

From what I heard and read Dad was an excellent baseball player. Mom always bragged about his ability and I remember reading in his yearbook from Franklin K. Lane High School about what a great player he was. His nickname was Powerhouse.

I remember him telling me how he wouldn't go to the movies because it was bad for his eyes, similar to stories I would read years later about Ted Williams. Dad originally attended Thomas Jefferson High School; until he found out they didn't have a baseball team. So, he transferred to Franklin K. Lane High School, where he became the starting centerfielder and clean-up hitter for Coach Bob Berman. Berman was a former Major League catcher, a contemporary of Babe Ruth and Ty Cobb, who appeared in two games in 1918 before the season, and his career were cut short by World War I. (The World Series was played in the first week of September that year, won by Ruth's Red Sox, the last title they would win for 86 years.) Like Moonlight Graham, whose story was included in *Field of Dreams*, Berman never made a plate appearance, but he did record two putouts catching the legendary Hall-of-Famer, Walter Johnson. Berman, a New York native and Fordham graduate, coached the Lane baseball team from 1937 to 1968, and I got to meet him when Dad arranged for the St. Gabriel's CYO (Catholic Youth Organization) team to play at Lane.

Throughout his teen years Dad played on several local teams, always playing with older kids to help develop and sharpen his skills. I have pictures of Dad playing at Dexter Park, which was right next to Franklin K. Lane High School, in Queens, just over the Brooklyn border. I remember him telling me that in 1933 he saw Babe Ruth play there, and how he played there as a teenager in 1939. I have also seen him in the uniform of the Indians Base Ball Club, which played in Highland Park. The story he liked to tell, more often than about seeing Ruth, was when he was playing centerfield and the ball was hit to leftfield, being played by his friend and neighbor Jerry. Jerry misplayed the ball, resulting in the ball hitting off Jerry's head into the air. Dad, backing him up, caught the ball on the fly, for an out.

In 1942, when he was eighteen years old, Dad had two tryouts, one with the Brooklyn Dodgers and one with the New York Yankees. The Dodgers' tryout was as a walk-on. I remember Dad telling me that the Dodgers called the walk-ons "donkeys." He always told me that Bobby Thomson, the New York Giant famous for hitting The Shot Heard 'Round the World to beat Ralph Branca and the Dodgers in 1951, was at that Dodger tryout with him in 1941. Years later, when I had the opportunity to introduce Dad to Thomson at a baseball alumni dinner, I'll be damned if Dad didn't ask him about that tryout and Thomson confirmed that he was there!

With the Yankees it was a different story. It seems like it is always a different story with the Yankees. Dad had been scouted by Paul Kritchell, a famous Yankee scout who signed Lou Gehrig in 1923 and who would sign Whitey Ford in 1947. Liking what he saw, Kritchell invited Dad to a tryout at Yankee Stadium. I remember Dad telling me that during his first tryout, at Yankee Stadium in the fall of 1942, he actually hit a couple of balls into the stands. He had tried out for centerfield, and they invited him to come back for a second tryout in the spring of 1943, but wanted him to work out at shortstop. They didn't feel he was tall enough for the outfield.

Dad was due to graduate high school in February 1943, and was to go back to the Stadium after that, when the Yankees returned from spring training. His fallback position was to attend St. John's University, which had recruited him to play ball. None of Dad's older brothers or sisters had graduated high school and my Aunt Ang, Dad's youngest sister, has told me of the discussion the family held about how it could possibly afford Dad's college tuition. Her memory is that Uncle Frank said the family would work at whatever it took to pay that tuition if Dad would be going to college. Well, the love was there, but there was no need for the tuition money, or the second trip to Yankee Stadium. Uncle Sam trumped Uncle Frank and took care of that. Upon arriving home from his high school graduation, Dad received a letter calling him to serve our country in World War II. Dad joined the United States Navy and as I wrote earlier, he served in the South Pacific, and earned medals for his service in Iwo Jima and Okinawa. On the morning of February 14, 1943, when Dad was to leave for the service, starting with a bus picking up the local recruits on New Lots Avenue, Uncle Sal, at the age of 12, saddened at the thought of his childhood idol going off to war, carried Dad's suitcase for him from 688 Essex to New Lots Avenue and waited with him for the bus.

After the war was over, so were Dad's chances of ever playing in the Major Leagues. He never lost his love for the game though, or his intensity in playing, teaching, coaching, or discussing it. Baseball was serious business for him. Looking back on it, I honestly feel he never got over the fact that he lost his opportunity to play in the Majors. He felt he was cheated by being denied his true destiny. He had survived the War and was grateful for that, as many did not, but he knew he had missed his chance and regretted it deeply. I didn't get all that as a kid, but as I got older and realized the regrets we have as adults, I am more and more convinced in my opinion that although he proudly answered his call to serve our country, he definitely resented that fate took him out of the lineup.

Looking back on it now, as an adult, I guess I can see that all of those experiences made Dad serious when it came to baseball. He taught Rob and I all the lingo of the game, like Texas Leaguer (a bloop single between the infield and outfield), a "cripple pitch" (when the count was 3 balls and 1 strike and the pitcher had to throw you a strike), double dip (a double play) and Uncle Charlie (a curveball). To pass time on occasion he would quiz us by giving us initials of a ballplayer and we would have to guess his name, or he would give us a player's nickname and we were expected to know who it was. I think I was the only third grader in Brooklyn in 1962 who knew that Paul Waner and Lloyd Waner were "Big Poison" and "Little Poison," respectively, Luke Appling was "Old Aches and Pains" and that Earl Averill was "The Earl of Snohomish."

One of the baseball stories that was a classic "stoop story" was Aunt Angie's recitation of Game 7 of the 1952 World Series. Aunt Connie got tickets to the game and she and Uncle Joe, Dad and Aunt Ang went to Ebbets Field, on October 7, 1952, to see if the Yankees could win their fourth straight championship against the Brooklyn Dodgers, who they had defeated in the fall classic in 1941, 1947 and 1949.

The Series was played over seven consecutive days, October 1 to October 7, with no "travel days", putting an emphasis on pitching. The Dodgers won Game 5 in 11 innings, taking a 3-2 lead in the Series and were looking to make 1952 the "next year" that Dodger fans were always waiting for, heading home to Ebbets Field and only needing to win one of the two games at home. The Yankees, behind the pitching of Vic ("The Springfield Rifle") Raschi (who was Italian as Aunt Ang would always remind us), and home runs from Yogi Berra and Mickey Mantle, won Game 6, 3-2, forcing a Game 7.

The Yankees started Eddie Lopat and the Dodgers started Joe Black. Neither was still in the game at the crucial moment in the bottom of the seventh inning. Powered by Mickey Mantle's home run and RBI single, the Yanks took a 4-2 lead into the bottom of the seventh. After Raschi, the Game 6 winner now pitching in relief, loaded the bases with one out, relief pitcher, Bob ("Sarge") Kuzava retired Duke ("The Duke of Flatbush") Snider on an infield pop fly to third base, but then had to face Jackie Robinson with the potential tying and go-ahead runs on base with two outs. Robinson lifted a wind-blown pop-up to the right side of the infield. Kuzava and the rest of the Yankee infield looked at first baseman Joe Collins. Collins, who apparently lost the ball in the sun, was looking back at them for help, and stood still, not knowing which way to run to the ball. As Aunt Ang tells it, she and my dad and all of the other 33,000+ fans were on their feet screaming: Yankee fans anxious for someone to catch the ball and end the scoring threat and the inning, and Dodger fans desperate to tie the game or take the lead in the crucial Game 7, and finally beat the Yanks.

From his position at second base, Billy Martin sprinted between the mound and first base. His cap flew off as he lunged forward to catch the ball at his shoe tops preserving the lead. The rest of the game was scoreless and the Yanks took home their fourth straight World Series championship, leaving my relatives a story to tell and re-tell.

When Rob and I were kids, Dad would take us for batting practice as often as possible. It seems now like that happened every day. There was a fenced-in area under the elevated trains on Elton Street (the "el"). Dad would always pitch, and Rob and I alternated between batting and playing third base. Every few minutes the roar of the train overhead would cause me to flinch and Dad would tell me to think of that noise as the crowd cheering for me and to get used to it. The ground was covered with all these large rocks, which I remember as being soaked with the oil that dripped from the trains above. There were no "true" bounces, and Dad was less than pleased if we hit the ball to the right side where there was no fielder. Rob and I both became dead pull right-handed hitters and pretty good fielders as a result of those batting practice experiences.

Dad's favorite drill for fielding practice was to play a game of Pepper, but he made it competitive and called it DONKEY. He would have a bat and stand in the bunting stance. Rob and I, and whoever else was there would stand about eight to ten feet away and throw the ball (overhand only, no lobbing!) to Dad. He would hit every pitch and could control who he hit it to. If you made an error you got a letter, first error you got a D, second error you got an O, third error you got an N, and so on, until a fielder got six errors, spelling DONKEY, causing his elimination. As players were eliminated, Dad would increase the tempo a little, so that when there were only two fielders left the competitive nature to win took over the drill. I used that drill for years with all the teams I coached.

Looking back on it now, it is apparent to me that Dad, having missed his chance at the Major Leagues, saw Rob and me as chances two and three. If it couldn't be him wearing a Major League uniform then it would be one of his sons. Rob bore the brunt of the pressure applied by Dad, especially since Dad coached Rob's teams. Being good enough wasn't good enough. Even winning wasn't good enough. We had to be perfect and that is a pretty difficult thing for a kid to do. I saw how important baseball was to Dad, and maybe that is why as a kid I dreamt of being a professional baseball player. But then again so did most kids who had any athletic ability at all.

Dad helped establish the baseball program at St. Gabriel's Church and as I said he coached Rob's team. I was only old enough to be the bat boy. But I distinctly remember my first uniform. That was 1958. They didn't have polyester or pull-over uniforms. We had the real deal – sanitary hose, stirrups, and scratchy flannel uniforms that had holes under the arms to allow your armpits to "breathe" and to keep you from dying, or at least stinking from perspiration. It wasn't anywhere near as glamorous as the uniforms we give to kids today. But I remember the joy I experienced when I got that first uniform. I didn't ever want to take it off. Dad made sure I got number 7, and I still have that uniform.

The only question I remember having was why we were the St. Gabriel's Cubs, with uniforms complete with the Chicago emblems, and not my Dad's favorites, the Yankees, or our hometown team, the Dodgers. Well, it turns out that one of the semi-pro teams that Dad played on, with Uncle Joe, was the Cubs, and I guess Dad had special memories of that team. So, Cubs we were.

Although we lived in Brooklyn, home of the famous wait-til-next-year Dodgers, we grew up as Yankee fans. I believe the genesis for that was Dad's having been scouted by the Yanks, and the fact that the Yanks were perennial winners, something on which Dad placed a great measure of importance. I also think it was helped along by the number of Italians on the Yankees: Joe DiMaggio, Phil Rizzuto, Yogi Berra, Vic Raschi and Tony Lazzeri. Aunt Ang has told me that the family would buy Wheaties just because Joe DiMaggio's picture was on a Wheaties box. The final straw was when the Dodgers and Giants abandoned New York for California, in 1958, leaving the Yanks as the only team in town until the Mets were born in 1962.

Thanks to Dad's love of the game, shared by the whole family, we got to see a lot of baseball. That was helped by our friendship with the Esposito family, who were the groundskeepers for Ebbets Field (before the Dodgers left) and who then took care of the field at Yankee Stadium.

Baseball was king in New York in the 1950s and early 60s. We loved playing it, but getting to see it live was something else, especially the Yanks who always seemed to be in the World Series. I can say I attended a Dodgers game at Ebbets Field, and, thanks to Uncle Sal, a Mets game at the Polo Grounds. Thanks to Aunt Ang, I met an acne-faced, teenage Mel Stottlemyre in 1964, and held Frank Crosetti's glove. One day, with Dad, Rob and cousin Frank, in the players' parking lot right across from the

Press Gate at the old Yankee Stadium, I saw Mickey Mantle climb into his white, convertible Cadillac with the license plate "MM-77." I shared so many other Yankee memories with my brother thanks to Dad, Aunt Ang and Uncle Sal.

We never missed a Yankee game on WPIX-TV (Channel 11) or on the radio. The broadcasting trio was one of the classics of all time: Red Barber, Mel Allen and Phil Rizzuto. Barber ("The Old Redhead"), born and raised in Mississippi, displayed a Southern accent and employed folksy figures of speech that were priceless. He would sign on with "This is the old redhead coming to you from the big ballpark in the Bronx." When things were going good for the Yanks he would say they were in the "catbird's seat" and seventy years later there is still discussion as to whether he or James Thurber made that phrase popular. I remember Rob and I laughing in the summer of 1966 when Barber commented on the situation Yankee pitcher Dooley Womack put himself in by walking two batters, saying "Womack's got one foot in the pickle barrel." That would be Barber's last year of broadcasting for the Yankees, where he started in 1954, after fourteen years of broadcasting Dodger games, and Cincinnati Reds games before that.

Mel Allen was another transplanted Southerner, born in Alabama, who started with the Yanks in 1939 and became the Voice of the New York Yankees. To this day, when I hear an announcer lamely broadcast a Yankee home run, my mind's voice superimposes Mel's mellifluous, classic "Going, going, it is gone! A Ballantine blast!" followed by his signature "How about that?" Years later, I got to meet Allen several times at Yankee Dutch Treat luncheons at Gallagher's. Every time I met him was a treat.

The third component of the crew was Phil Rizzuto, who added that Italian, New York-centric, homey feel that made you sense you were watching or listening to the game with your own Uncle Phil. He made it okay to call someone a "huckleberry" and to eat cannoli while broadcasting the game. (When I was lucky enough to attend the Phil Rizzuto Golf Tournament in New Jersey as Ryne Duren's guest, I was thrilled to be able to deliver a box of cannoli to Rizzuto.)

Back then the same three announcers did TV and radio, moving from booth to booth every three innings, so over a season, and the seasons, you knew from their comments on TV exactly what they were describing when they were on radio.

I remember the day I attended the Yankees' first Bat Day. My dad was coaching Rob's Tyro Team and I was playing for Mr. Miller's Juniors. We were at the same park north of Linden Boulevard (between Fountain Avenue and Euclid Avenue) on catty-corner fields, and I was scheduled to start my very first game as a pitcher. I did well for the first two innings, and when Dad looked across the field in the top of the third inning I wasn't on the mound. He came over to see if I got knocked out of the game only to learn that Aunt Ang showed up with Yankee tickets and I left! At the Stadium, we all got Little League-size reproduction bats from Louisville Slugger, and every time the Yankees were up we held up the bats, like 50,000 exclamation points, to our chant of "WE WANT A HIT!" Our devotion was rewarded when in the bottom of the ninth inning Hector Lopez, #11, delivered a game-winning hit, known today as a walk-off hit.

Thanks to Aunt Ang I also got to enjoy a bunch of games sitting in the hanging boxes, a special series of seats meant for members of the press, in the "old" Yankee Stadium that were suspended from the Loge section along the third base line. One of the most special games was on Saturday, October 3, 1964. Rob and I were with Aunt Ang sitting in the hanging boxes when Al Downing and the Yankees took the field against the Cleveland Indians with a chance to clinch the 1964 American League Pennant. (I checked the box scores, and believe it or not only 14,879 fans were in the stands that day.) I was immediately rewarded and thrilled when my hero, Mickey Mantle, hit a double in the bottom of the first inning to knock in two runs and put the Yanks ahead. But the Indians came back and by the bottom of the eighth, Downing was gone and the score was tied at 3-3. They Yanks scored five times in the bottom of the eighth, and we were still in those hanging boxes when Pedro Ramos delivered a pitch to Vic Davalillo who popped up in foul territory off third base, and the Yanks clinched. It was the Yanks' fifth straight pennant and a chase that doesn't get the credit it deserves. On September 16th of that year the Yanks were in third place and went on an eleven game winning streak that put them in first place to stay. It was that year and that pennant race, and that clinching game that secured my heart for baseball forever.

Scorecards were 25 cents and when you went to a game with Dad you kept score. The yearbook was $1. It was a special treat, once a year, when Dad had the money and treated us to a yearbook. It had a page for each of the stars and a half a page for the non-starters, and had pictures of the players' families and great moments from the previous year. Rob and I would read it from cover to cover and it took a cherished place on the bookshelf every year. I still have some of them. I really can't imagine there is a kid today who looks forward to the yearbook the way we did, or who cherished it as much. They were simple $1 souvenirs that we treasured.

I lost track of how many times Rob and I watched Gary Cooper's portrayal of Lou Gehrig in *Pride of the Yankees*, but I can guarantee it was every time that it aired. I didn't think a movie could get better than that. But in 1961, the year of the historic home run battle between Roger Maris and Mickey Mantle which culminated in Maris breaking Babe Ruth's record, Maris, Mantle and Yogi Berra had small roles in a Doris Day movie, *A Touch of Mink*. And then they came out with *Safe at Home*, a movie **featuring** Mantle and Maris. Shortly thereafter Mom and Dad bought me Joe Garagiola's book, *Baseball Is a Funny Game*, and I soon learned that I could not only fall in love with a sport, but with books about sports.

Having taken the time to consider my relationship with baseball as a whole to write this chapter, I fully understand why it means so much to me still. It was a game that captured my father's attention, which he excelled at and aspired to make a career of. It was part of our household in Brooklyn, and it holds a special meaning from the times and memories given to be my by Dad, Aunt Ang, Uncle Sal and many others.

After my dad passed away, in 2000, the Town Board of the Town of Oyster Bay, at the direction of Supervisor John Venditto, named the local youth baseball field, Pops Sabellico Field. It was a special honor since Dad had been to that field many times, helping me coach Chris and Jim.

Since that time the field is commonly referred to as Pops Park. Several years later, a local Boy Scout, as part of his Eagle Scout project, planted a rose garden in the right field foul area, and there is a plaque the dedicating the garden to my mom, Rose.

ONIONS IN HOT SAUCE

What's baseball without hot dogs? Baseball was Dad's favorite sport and hot dogs were his favorite meal. I remember him always saying "Some days you eat steak and some days you eat hot dogs" to teach us that you don't win every day, but I think if he had a choice he would opt for the hot dogs. Which reminds me of Humphrey Bogart's famous line "A hot dog at the ballpark is better than steak at the Ritz." Dad's favorite way to eat the franks was boiled, or steamed, topped with brown mustard, and sauerkraut or onions in hot sauce. Credit for this recipe goes to my cousin Antoinette, who now goes by Toni, but who we all know as "Noots."

3 lbs. white onions, sliced
Olive oil
Crushed red pepper
Salt
Pepper
4 cloves garlic, diced
4 shakes soy sauce
4 shakes Gravy Master
4 shakes worchestire sauce
Heinz Ketchup

Place sliced onions, garlic, crushed red pepper, salt, and pepper in frying pan, add enough olive oil to fry, not too much; Cook, stirring constantly until onions are transparent, but not wrinkled – do not let onions get wrinkled or cooked too much;

Take frying pan off heat, remove majority of oil, add Gravy Master, soy sauce, and worchestire sauce; stir;

Add Heinz ketchup until all onions are coated in brownish red sauce; return to very low heat to cook down ketchup – approximately eight to ten minutes.

These are also great served with a burger or steak.

Rob and I with our St. Gabriel's Cubs Uniforms. He was a player and I was a batboy.

Pops Sabellico Park, Farmingdale, Town of Oyster Bay, New York.

Maria Milza and me.   *Johnny Chisefsky and me.*

Group of kids on Essex Street, left to right: Maria Milza, Carol Ann Taylor, Joyce Milza, Peter Puglisi, Janet Puglisi, me, and John Chisefsky. The dog is Terry, the Puglisi's Jack Russell Terrier.

CHAPTER 5

KINDERGARTEN

I raised my children on Long Island, New York, where the social and educational environment dictated that by age three they were already engaged in some form of structured learning, like "Library School." In fact, my youngest, born eight years after my oldest, was in a Nursery School at just over two years of age. That was not the educational landscape that faced us in Brooklyn during my childhood, at least not from what I can remember. The first formal educational experience was Kindergarten, and they didn't offer that in the parochial school, only in the public school.

At the age of five I was old enough to go to Kindergarten, although at that time I thought everybody was saying "kinder garden" and I was going somewhere where they had flowers and tomato plants. I had no idea I was going into a classroom setting with some kids I really didn't know. What I remember is being brought to Public School 202 (PS 202 in New York speak), the big brick impersonal building known in our neighborhood simply as "202." All I knew about that building at that time was three things: 1) it had a caged-in area on its roof, which I really didn't understand (and years later found out that because of space shortage, that's where the kids went to play during physical education classes); 2) it was where my parents went to vote, although at that time I didn't know what voting was, but only that my parents went there every so often, and went into a booth in private; and 3) it was where the kids who didn't go to Catholic school went to school, and my immature brain interpreted that to mean this is where the different kids were.

My memories of my Kindergarten career in "202" consist of one session of finger painting, crying hysterically for my parents, and being very, very upset. This first foray into the world of being separated from one's parents so that the world could help educate me did not go very swimmingly. I missed my toys. I missed my grandmother. I missed my brother. I missed my room. I wasn't ready for the world of formal education yet. And I must have been quite upset, because I don't ever remember going back to Kindergarten. The experience may have lasted more than one day, but if it did, I have no recollection of anything other than the finger painting effort and the hysteria.

CHAPTER 6

TUFFY

Just a short time after the Kindergarten experiment we had the pet dog experiment, which failed even more miserably than Kindergarten. All of my dad's brothers, but not him, worked in the stuffed toy business. Needless to say, there was always a load of stuffed toys in our apartment while we grew up; and thanks to my uncles, every girl Rob or I ever dated or thought about dating got at least one sleepy doll, or stuffed animal, complete with wind-up music box that usually played Brahms' Lullaby. Some of the toys were very, very special. When Rob was very young, like 5, he had his tonsils removed and when Uncle Joey visited him in the hospital he gave him a stuffed monkey. Rob named it Aba-Daba, because of the popular song "Aba-Daba Honeymoon" recorded by Debbie Reynolds in 1954. To this day, I still have a stuffed Santa with red corduroy suit and leather boots that Uncle Joey gave me.

All that being said, by the time Rob was eight and I was five, Dad thought it was time that we should have a live animal, a pet dog. Enter Tuffy, an Alaskan Husky.

I guess my father's real thoughts were that the dog would be a great pet for my brother who was 8 at the time, and truly, as a dad, I believe that every youngster should have a pet. There seems to be a special bond between a young boy and a dog, especially his first puppy. Well, Tuffy and Rob were getting along splendidly as well as I can remember. To me, however, Tuffy was an animated stuffed animal, and none of the other stuffed animals had the slightest bit of trouble with me poking them in the eye or playing roughly with them, so I acted the same way with Tuffy. Well, Tuffy may have been his name, but the general feeling in the household was that I was being too rough with the puppy and that either I was going to hurt him, or, in self-defense, the dog would snap and hurt me. Either way, the decision was that

Tuffy had to go, and for years I questioned if the decision would have been so easy if there existed a Bide-a-Wee for five year old boys. If my brother had been given a vote the dog would have stayed and I would have been put up for adoption. Even after fifty years this remained a very sore spot. I didn't dare mention the word Tuffy in Rob's presence, and I found a way to look away or quickly change the subject, should an Alaskan Husky enter our view, or our discussion, at any time.

Within a year or so after the Tuffy incident, we moved down the block (the wrong way on a one way street, which always seemed humorous to me), into a first floor apartment in the four-family house owned by my maternal grandparents. Don't think it odd that both my sets of grandparents lived on the same block. Brooklyn in the late 1950s was that way, sort of an urban Amish thing. Families stayed together; some in the same neighborhood, some on the same block, some in the same house, some in the same apartment. Besides my grandparents, four sets of Sabellico aunts and uncles and seven first cousins all lived on the same block. Anyway, as it relates to the dog story, living in my maternal grandparents' house was altogether different as I will explain later, but suffice it to say that pets were not allowed, and that made Rob even angrier at me because having lost his chance to keep Tuffy he wouldn't get a dog again until we left Brooklyn, and by then he was already sixteen, and almost a MAN.

Just as we were about to leave Brooklyn, Joe and Lena Verga's dog. Toby, had a litter, and we got to keep one. It was a beagle, and Dad named it Pepper, because of his salt-and-pepper markings, but maybe because of his love for our fielding drill.

Rob and me with Santa Claus, 1955.

CHAPTER 7

CHRISTMAS

THE CHRISTMAS ROOM

Grandpa Sisto's house at 688 Essex was a two-family home and the second floor apartment we lived in was slightly larger than the first-floor apartment to the extent that there was a small room in our apartment, above the vestibule. That room was sort of out of the way, adjacent to my parent's bedroom in the front of the apartment and only accessible from the hallway. My brother and I shared a bedroom, with twin beds, in the back of the apartment, behind the kitchen and bathroom.

We only lived at 688 until I was six, but I have the clearest, dearest, fondest memory of that little room. It was a room usually used by my parents for storage, and as a six year old that room was off limits to me. As I remember, the "off-limits" rule was strictly enforced beginning about Thanksgiving, and I came to realize that the little room was our North Pole, where Santa's elves stored the goodies we would be getting for Christmas.

One night in early December, I guess the thoughts of sugarplums dancing in my head led to "ants in my pants" as Mom would describe it, making me kind of hyperactive, which was never a good thing when Dad wasn't in the mood. That led to me crying, which created a need for Mom to divert my attention to save my life. It must have been bad because she told me she was going to let me in on a special secret, and it was in the little room. Only she and I went in and there were was a large box she opened which contained four or five presents she had bought for my dad. I got to see the presents before anyone else, and together we wrapped them in shiny paper with pictures of Santa Claus and snowmen. I forgot all about my dad's anger, lost in the privilege of being in a special place with Mom with advance access to Christmas presents. That moment, in that room for probably twenty minutes, over fifty years ago, has never left me, and every Christmas, as we all start to hide presents in special nooks and crannies throughout the house, my mind brings me right back into that room, with my mom there to protect me.

THE CHRISTMAS PLAY

In most parts of the world the portion of the Bible that is most often portrayed in theatrical fashion is the Passion of Christ, detailing His Crucifixion and Resurrection. While the priests and nuns did instill in us the significance of Easter as the most important religious holiday in the Catholic faith, somehow their actions were contrary to their words, and it came through loud and clear to all of us that Christmas was the real deal. We would come to learn that the salvation of man was based on the death and resurrection of Christ, but to us kids a couple of colored Easter eggs, a chocolate bunny and some plastic grass was dwarfed, big time, by a Christmas tree, lights, snow, toy trains, unbelievable pastries and foods, Christmas carols, and, oh yeah, presents.

One of the staples of the Christmas season when you attended Catholic school was the Nativity Play. The privilege of being a cast member went to the eighth graders, while all of the other students comprised the audience, along with proud parents, grandparents, aunts and uncles. The play was performed twice, once during the weekly Assembly for all the students and once in an evening performance for the general public.

It would seem that on Christmas, Jesus would be the star of the show, but it was a non-speaking role and all of those auditioning were too old for the part, so the "leads" were Mary and Joseph. If you were selected to play the Virgin Mary or Joseph, it was as if you were being pre-ordained for a special role in life.

The stage in the school auditorium, which was used for Mass on Sunday mornings, was transformed into the stable area which housed the famous manger which served as Baby Jesus' first crib. In a total mix of seasonal symbols, both sides of the stage were bookended by large artificial Christmas trees, decorated with garland and ornaments by a parishioner, Mr. Vito Torres, who worked for Macy's. I remember that the ornaments were large and each was just a single color, much different from those at home. The play started with Mary and Joseph travelling from the rear of the auditorium up the middle aisle, representing their flight from Egypt, as a narrator told their story. After they took their places on the stage, the shepherds came in, and eventually the Three Wise Men. All of this was accompanied by the school chorus, singing the appropriate songs, led by Sister Saint Agatha and her magic pitch pipe. After the play was over, the chorus continued to entertain the crowd with the Christmas carols that didn't fit into the play, like *Rudolph the Red Nosed Reindeer* and *Frosty the Snowman*.

The Nativity Play was cancelled the year I was in the eighth grade. The joke in school was that Mary and Joseph finally found room at the inn, a joke which earned you a job at erasing the blackboards if the nuns heard you. Actually it was cancelled because of the illness of Sister Marie Fontbonne, the eighth grade nun, and we had enough to do to keep up with actual school work. However, three years earlier, when Rob was in the eighth grade, he was selected to play the role of a shepherd. I remember the staff that my mom and dad created for him to walk with, and the robes my mom made for him to wear. You would not believe the fanfare that went into the preparation for that performance. To my knowledge, there are no films of that performance, or even still shots, but it is as clear in my mind as the picture I now see on my 60" High Def Television. There was Rob, walking on stage into the stable containing the manger where Baby Jesus lay! A Kodak moment if ever there was one!

LA VIGILIA

Italian families, in Brooklyn at least, referred to Christmas Eve as *La Vigilia*, The Vigil. Traditionally, the feast that we consumed on Christmas Eve was meatless, and featured a huge variety of fish and seafood the likes of which you only saw and tasted once a year. Depending on the ritual that your parents or grandparents brought with them from Italy to Brooklyn, the number of seafood dishes your family prepared was either seven or nine. The seven represented the seven sacraments and the number nine was the Trinity multiplied by three; I don't really know why it was multiplied by three, but I guess that three dishes would never be enough feasting for any respectable Italian family, and if you multiplied the Trinity by two, it left you with six, and you appeared to be less than the families who were enjoying seven.

The family always took turns hosting different holidays, but all the time we lived in Brooklyn, and for years afterwards, Christmas Eve was exclusively hosted by my parents. Dad was the main cook when it came to the seafood. The actual seafood dishes comprising the seven or nine fishes were different at every family's celebration, and sometimes from year to year, but there were always staples that were present every Christmas Eve, including baccalà (dried cod fish) and calamari (squid). Baccalà was always a fun word to say as a kid, but it was serious business to the adults. As always, Dad took the holiday and the preparation of food as a teaching opportunity. We went with him to the fish market on Blake Avenue and Cleveland Street (whose catty-corner front door was always guarded on either side by a huge bushel of live snails). He would explain to Rob and me that baccalà was the Italian name for dried, salted cod fish, that it was originally salted to preserve it prior to the invention of refrigeration, and that cod fish was the most widely eaten fish in the world. He said the process of salting fish to preserve it dated back hundreds of years; that it was the world's oldest known preservation method, and it could keep fish preserved and edible for several years. Preparing the baccalà was a long process. It involved soaking it for several days, changing the water every so often. Eventually most, but not all, of the salt washed away, leaving a fleshy fish infused with a great savory taste.

The night of Christmas Eve and the memories of all of the Christmas Eves of my childhood are special beyond my ability to convey. The night was filled with family, love, food, fun, music, cards, games and anticipation. The room was filled with aunts, uncles, brothers, sisters, in-laws, moms, dads, grandmas and grandpas. There was always something happening, and it wasn't canned music or entertainment from the television. It was family members telling stories, reciting poems and singing songs. It might be cousin Libby, an amateur ventriloquist, entertaining us with her dummies, Irving and Max. ("What's your name?" *"Max."* "Max what?" *"Max no difference!"*)

Once-a-year recipes came to life, as dish after dish came out of the kitchen. Shrimp, calamari, scungilli, clams, crabs, flounder, baccalà, etc. But no meat. Not until midnight. At midnight, everyone exchanged kisses and wishes of Merry Christmas, and then the second wave of food came out: sausages and peppers, lard bread, hams, etc. And then came the desserts and the fried dough. The fried dough was a treat that my family repeats to this day every Christmas. Sometime during the day Mom would make several batches of pizza dough and it would rise in bowls covered with towels, punched down every so often. When it came time for dessert, the fried dough was the main event. They would tear off pieces of the dough and drop it into boiling oil. Sometimes they would wrap the dough around a piece of apple, or mozzarella cheese. The plain ones and the apple ones would be drizzled with honey. Fig pudding be damned!

OTHER CHRISTMAS MEMORIES

Although the feast of the fishes seems to be a central memory, and continuing tradition, for many Italian Americans, my memories of the Christmases of my youth, while including the smells and tastes of that fish feast, are much richer and deeper than that. Christmas was more than just a religious holiday, and it was so much more than just one day or night. It just seemed like everybody was in a good mood, not just the Catholics and

Christians. The older, cynical version of me tells me that it was the cash register ringing after Thanksgiving with Christmas shopping sales that made everybody happy, but my nostalgic side remembers it much differently.

Every store had a special display, from something as simple as a string of lights in the window and a small Christmas tree to the grand display of a Macy's or Gimbels. And it was truly special because it was for a limited time. It didn't start right after Halloween like it does now. Thanksgiving was given its due and then, and only then, did everybody ramp up for Christmas. My mother, my grandmother, all my aunts, and probably every other Italian housewife in the area broke out the special holiday recipes and started baking up a storm. Struffoli, bowties, pizzelles, special cookies and cakes were popping out of Brooklyn kitchens at a rapid rate. One Italian specialty which clearly signaled the coming of Christmas was Struffoli (Honey Balls). That was a production: making the dough, cutting the little squares, frying them in oil, then re-frying them in honey, in a special frying pan that was my mother's grandmother's. The people who created those recipes either had a lot more time on their hands or were much more patient than we are today.

The Mario Lanza, Ray Conniff Singers, and Johnny Mathis Christmas albums, with Johnny in his ski outfit, were dusted off and played endlessly on the victrola, along with two special 45s that everybody seemed to own: Gene Autry singing *Rudolph the Red Nosed Reindeer* and Burl Ives singing *Have a Holly Jolly Christmas*. In school, the nuns allowed us to decorate the classroom with construction paper cutouts of the manger and the Star of the East. The front windows of every apartment displayed the various holiday stencils we made with pink Glass Wax, and you were really good if you could fit the stencil of Santa and his whole team of reindeer rising into the sky into one of the apartment's double-hung windows. It seemed like the Coca Cola version of Santa Claus, which we all believed was the most realistic, was everywhere. Toy trains circled almost every Christmas tree, and it was a special treat to blow the train's horn by pressing the red button on the transformer, and making the locomotive smoke by placing one of those small aspirin-like tablets into it. We got special coloring books and our older cousins showed us how to stay within the lines and how to highlight the characters we colored with a deeper shade. And we were "allowed" to cut those pages out of the book and post them on the walls of the rumpus room as decorations for the Christmas Eve party.

Another Christmas tradition was cooking rabbit, a treat we only had once a year. One of the neighborhood families, the Ciappas, raised rabbits, and every Christmas, Dad would order a rabbit, which Mr. Ciappa would deliver already "dressed" which is an unusual term because it had the exact opposite meaning you would normally attribute to the word. Dad would be in charge of cooking the rabbit, and it brings back a couple of specific memories: Dad would always refer to the rabbit by the German name: Hasenpfeffer, just because I think he liked to say the word, and secondly, it was the first food that I remember being accompanied by the phrase: "it tastes just like chicken" to everyone Dad tried to entice into trying to taste it.

By the time Christmas Eve came, we were already out of school for a few days and in a party mood. At some point we got to take a ride into Manhattan, which was a treat in itself, and got to visit the "real" Santa at Macy's and tell him in person what you really wanted for Christmas. Every closet was full of tins of special cookies and treats. The baccalà was soaking somewhere. You were busting to have your parents open the gift that you got for them with "your own money" and had wrapped and hidden somewhere secret, but the real anticipation that had you jumping out of your skin was having to wait to open the presents that Santa was bringing. The Christmas ornaments were resurrected from the basement, leading to the annual battles of determining which lights worked and which ones didn't and who got to put the "special" ornaments on the tree, including the one with the water in it that bubbled after it had warmed up and you flicked it with your finger. And everybody was happy.

There was another constant of Christmas that had to do with Ozone Park, Queens and not East New York, Brooklyn. That was the visit to Uncle Frank and Aunt Nellie's house on the night that the fire department was driving Santa Claus around to visit all the kids in the neighborhood. You would wait on their front stoop for what seemed like forever as you heard the fire trucks making their rounds through the neighborhood. Then as they turned the corner your pulse quickened as you caught sight of Santa and you ran to the curb to get a closer look. It was over in a flash, the bag of hard Christmas candy he tossed to you lasted a few days, but the memories of those spice flavored candies and those special moments are still as strong as ever.

FRIED CALAMARI
CALAMARI FRITTO

What would Christmas be without the food feast that was the seven fishes? And the family's favorite was always the fried calamari. Dad was always looking for ways to make it tastier, and crisp, not chewy. He finally settled on this recipe, and always insisted on frying it at the last minute, so it could be enjoyed fresh from the hot oil. I can taste it now. It brings back the magic of Christmas Eve, the loving feeling of those parties, and Dad's satisfied smile as the family sat down to eat the fried calamari while it was red hot.

1 pound calamari, cleaned, sliced into rings (leave tentacles whole)
2 cups buttermilk
1 cup flour
½ teaspoon salt
Oil for frying

Clean and slice the calamari, rinse with cold water and place in a bowl with the buttermilk.

Refrigerate.

Mix flour and salt in a small bowl.

Place vegetable oil in a deep fryer and heat oil to 400 degrees.

Take a handful of calamari at a time, shake off all of the excess liquid and toss it in the flour. Then place in the fry basket and fry for three or four minutes until golden brown.

Remove and drain off all excess oil, and salt to taste. The perfect complement to the fried calamari is Brother Rob's

Hot Sauce, which recipe immediately follows. If the sauce is too hot or you are just in the mood for a change, just squeeze some fresh lemon on the calamari and sprinkle with salt.

BROTHER ROB'S HOT SAUCE

Fried Calamari being one of Dad's favorites it was no wonder he loved working near Little Italy, where he could get great calamari at either Vincent's or The Limehouse. He made it a passion to duplicate the hot sauce they served, and he and my brother kept tinkering with it. Eventually Rob nailed it, and as a reward he got the job of preparing it every Christmas Eve. It is perfect on the Fried Calamari and served with Scungilli. But even those who don't like seafood, like my wife, Paula, love this sauce on linguine.

Olive oil
8 cloves of garlic, chopped
6 12 ounce cans tomato paste
2 12 ounce cans tomato sauce
3/4 cup sugar
Crushed red pepper flakes

Add a generous amount of olive oil to a large frying pan until oil is approximately one-half inch deep. Add chopped garlic and sauté until garlic is lightly browned.

Reduce to medium heat. Add tomato paste and tomato sauce, stirring constantly. Then add sugar and red pepper (to taste). Continue stirring over medium heat for approximately 15 minutes.

(The more hot pepper you add the closer you should keep the Brioschi.)

NOTE: This is a "double" recipe. Half of this recipe is just right for a large can of La Monica sliced scungilli and some pasta.

INSALATA FRUTTI DI MARE

1 pound shrimp (20 to 24 per lb.), peeled and deveined
1 pound squid, cleaned and cut into rings and pieces
1 pound bay scallops
1 large can sliced scungilli
½ cup olive oil
Juice of four fresh lemons
2 stalks celery, sliced
3 garlic cloves, minced
4 cherry peppers, hot or sweet, depending on your taste, sliced, with seeds removed
2 tablespoons flat-leaf parsley, finely chopped
1 teaspoon salt
Black pepper

Bring a large pot of salted water to a boil over high heat. Set a bowl of ice water nearby. Boil shrimp just until pink, about two minutes. Strain the shrimp and place them in the ice water.

Then place squid into boiling water and cook until the flesh is opaque, 45 seconds to one minute. Drain well, pat dry, and add to shrimp in ice water.

Repeat process with bay scallops. Drain and rinse scungilli. Drain the water from all seafood, and place the cooked seafood in a large bowl.

Add olive oil, lemon juice, garlic, parsley, celery, cherry peppers, salt and black pepper. Let salad marinate at room temperature for approximately two hours, tossing occasionally.

Before serving, taste the salad, and add fresh lemon juice or salt if necessary.

AUNT JEANNIE & AUNT ANGIE'S CHEESECAKE

Aunt Jeannie and Aunt Angie are our family's answer to Lucy and Ethel. The only difference was that they sort of alternated on who played the straight man. They became friends at the age of twelve, and after Aunt Jean married Uncle Sal, she became a member of the Sabellico family. That continued the relationship with Aunt Angie and it has endured for more than 70 years. When the family moved out to Long Island from Brooklyn, Aunt Ang and Uncle Sal and Aunt Jean bought a home together in Merrick, in 1966. After Uncle Sal passed away in 2002, the Aunts continued their decades-old relationship as it originally started: just the two of them. You knew that holiday occasions were special when a cheesecake was part of it, and especially the cheesecake that the Aunts made. Aunt Angie always kidded that everyone called this specialty Aunt Jeannie's Cheesecake, and that she did all the work, like crushing the crackers, etc. So, in honor of their special relationship, and their special place in my heart, and the work that Aunt Ang did, and in memory of all those special occasions when we enjoyed this treat, I give you this recipe as Aunt Jeannie & Aunt Angie's Cheesecake.

1 ½ cups crushed Zwieback crackers
2 tablespoons sugar
½ cup melted butter
16 oz. cream cheese
1 cup sugar
5 eggs, separated
2 cups sour cream
1 teaspoon vanilla extract
1 teaspoon lemon juice

Combine crushed Zwieback crumbs, sugar and melted butter. Press mixture into sides and bottom of 9 inch Springform pan.

Preheat oven to 350 degrees.

Soften cream cheese. Add sugar and egg yolks to cream cheese. Beat until light. Add sour cream, vanilla and lemon juice. Mix well.

In separate bowl, beat egg whites until stiff, not dry. Then fold beaten egg whites into cream cheese mixture, and pour into pan.

Bake at 350 for five minutes; then lower oven temperature to 250 and bake for an additional 65 minutes. Turn off oven, and open door, leaving cake in oven to cool slowly.

Refrigerate.

GRANDMA MILLIE'S COOKIES

This is a simple cookie recipe from my Grandma's kitchen. However, it is as enduring as it is simple. These little braids of dough compete with all the other fancy cookies at Christmas time as the kids' favorites, and that may very well be because my mom took the time to make these cookies with the kids.

2 sticks of butter (room temperature)
2 eggs
¾ cup sugar
3 ¼ cups flour
2 teaspoons baking powder
2 teaspoons almond extract

Mix all ingredients together, kneading until smooth. Roll pieces of dough into "snake like" rods, about six or seven inches long, and then shape into braids, about finger length. Bake on ungreased, non-stick cookie sheet in a 400 degree oven until the cookies start to brown, approximately 9 to 10 minutes.

Makes approximately 36 cookies.

You can make these cookies a little more festive by adding green or red food coloring to them, for the holidays, or you can get creative with toppings: either ice them with frosting, or a lemon glaze, or top them with melted chocolate and sprinkles.

MOM'S CHRISTMAS DATE COOKIES

These cookies are special to me because I remember making them with my mom, and I remember that when this recipe came out Christmas was not far behind. The dough needs to be made a day ahead of time and refrigerated overnight. I thought you should know that now and not when you get done with the dough expecting to then make the cookies right away. These cookies resemble homemade ravioli when they are done, and part of the process is cutting the dough into circles, using a drinking glass, and then, after they are filled, folding them over and sealing the edges with a fork. My brother and I would get the jobs of cutting the circles and sealing the cookies. I don't know that there is anything special about these cookies that makes them Christmas cookies, other than that is when my family made them, and tradition is a hard thing to argue with. Buon Natale!

Crust:
2/3 cup margarine
½ cup sugar
1 egg
3 tablespoons milk
¼ teaspoon vanilla
2 cups flour

Cream shortening and sugar; add egg, milk and vanilla. Then add flour and mix well. Refrigerate overnight.

Filling:
¼ cup chopped walnuts
½ cup chopped dates
½ cup raisins
3 tablespoons lemon juice

1 tablespoon honey
1 ½ teaspoons margarine

Cook together in saucepan until sticky.

Roll dough out on floured cutting board and cut into circles with rim of drinking glass. Put approximately one teaspoon of filling in the center of each circle. Fold circle over and seal seam by pressing down with fork tines.

Bake at 375 for approximately 12 minutes.

Makes approximately 36 cookies.

STRUFFOLI
HONEY BALLS

This is the quintessential Italian baked good to accompany that special cup of black coffee and Anisette around the Christmas holiday. You know as a child that a recipe is special when it involves using a cooking vessel that is kept in the basement all year and used only for this recipe. And when that special frying pan, with the very long handle, is brought upstairs every year, you heard the story about how it belonged to my mother's grandmother, and the recipe we were using to make the honey balls was her recipe. The story never varied, and neither did the Honey Balls. They were a project to make: a tribute to the patience of those who first came up with the idea. This involves several stages: making the dough, rolling out long "snakes"; cutting them into little pieces; frying the pieces in hot oil; re-frying them in honey (in the special frying pan); and then forming them into wreaths and adding nonpareils, all the while trying desperately not to burn your hands. Since my mom passed away I have made these several times. I have had them from several different bakeries, but they are just not the same.

6 cups flour
9 eggs
¾ teaspoon salt
4 cups oil
3 cups honey
1 ½ cups sugar

Place the flour on a large cutting board and create a well in the center of the flour. Add four eggs and half the salt to the well and knead; add the remaining eggs and salt and knead the dough until smooth. Allow the dough to rest for ten or fifteen minutes.

120

Pour oil into the deep fryer and preheat to 350 degrees.

Using a rolling pin and wax paper, roll the dough out until it is approximately ¼" thick. You can then either cut the dough into ½" strips, or take a piece of the dough and roll them into long chains or "snakes" as we called them, approximately ¼" to ½" in diameter. Then cut the "snakes" into ½" pieces.

Drop the pieces into the deep fryer a few at a time and cook until they are a light golden brown, turning them with a long wooden spoon. (The length of the spoon doesn't make a difference in the recipe, but it will keep your hand further away from the boiling oil.) The first batch of pieces will not be as dark as the remainder. Remove the pieces from the oil and drain well on plates lined with paper towels.

After all of the pieces have been deep fried, combine the honey and the sugar in a large frying pan and bring to a boil over a low heat, stirring constantly.

Add the fried pieces to the frying pan, a few handfuls at a time, and cook them in the honey, coating them completely. They should only be in the honey/sugar mixture for a minute or two.

Remove the coated pieces and place them on a cutting board. Then, careful not to burn your hands, arrange the pieces into mounds or a wreath, and decorate with nonpareils. Some people add candied cherries or almond pieces.

The assembled "honey balls" will last the entire holiday season if stored in a cool, dry place, and are a welcome treat when you bring them with you on holiday visits.

FRIED DOUGH
PIZZA FRITA

No Christmas Eve was complete until the dough was fried, and although a good amount of it was consumed that night, there was always a lot left for Christmas morning, probably because of the vast amount of other items that were eaten on Christmas Eve, and because my family's recipes were for large batches of food. The way I remember it, fried dough was another one of those peasant foods that lent itself to the family's creativity, or more likely, whatever was in the house at the time it was being made, as to what the dough could be stuffed or topped with.

Begin by making Pizza Dough, (see my recipe, earlier in the book), or by purchasing the dough from your local pizzeria. My grandparents and parents always made the dough, but to be honest to save time and work I have purchased the dough and sacrificed a little authenticity for convenience.

Fill a deep fryer to the fill line with vegetable oil. (My grandparents didn't have an electric deep fryer, so it was a cast iron frying pan that I remember as the cooking vessel for these treats.) Heat the oil to 400 degrees.

Test the oil for readiness by placing a very small piece of the dough into the oil. If it rises to the top, the oil is sufficiently hot.

Here's where the creativity and fun come into play. What you place into the dough before frying it, and what you put on the dough after it is fried, is limited only by your appetite, your imagination, and what is in the house at the time. A few examples:

Plain: Just twist off a piece of dough and place it in the oil, when it is golden brown scoop it out, drain the oil out of the spoon, and place the dough in bowl. You can leave it plain, or sprinkle granulated sugar on it, or drizzle honey on it.

Classic: The way we enjoyed it most, was to place a chunk of apple inside the dough and then stretch the dough to close it before placing it in the oil. Drizzle with honey when done and enjoy.

The most common other versions included stuffing the dough with either mozzarella cheese or anchovies. The cheese tends to leak out if you don't seal the dough well enough. And if you are going to try the anchovy version, do them last because the oil will make everything else after that taste like anchovies.

CHAPTER 8

CATHOLIC SCHOOL – PART I

FIRST GRADE – SISTER ANNA WILLETTA

In addition to Essex Street being special because so many of my family members lived on my block, the Catholic School had just been built on the corner, adjacent to our house, and I would be one of the first classes to enter in the first grade. Attached to the school was a convent, where the nuns lived. I was taught by the Sisters of St. Joseph, who wore flowing black robes, with a very stiff white bib and a black headpiece with a white triangle over the forehead, which I guess signified the Holy Trinity. I never quite understood the need for the starched white bib, but knowing I was a bit apprehensive about entering school, my brother told me that under that bib the nuns had a special piece of machinery that had an insert in it for every kid in their class, and that by checking that piece of machinery they would know exactly where I was and what I was doing and saying at all times, even when I was home.

Knowing what I know now, the technology for that type of a machine didn't exist then, although it would not surprise me if it existed now. Nonetheless, back then I believed my brother, and that made me afraid of the nuns. In fact, it made me a little nuts to think that they knew exactly what I was doing, when I was playing, eating, going to the …; well, you get the idea. When I exhibited my fear with a bout of hysteria, it led to Dad finding out about my brother's story, which led to a beating for Rob. That sort of backfired for him, but, to tell the truth, every so often the thought that the nuns knew my whereabouts and conduct at all times would come back to me, and I never forgot it.

In my first grade class there were approximately seventy-five students. We were extremely overcrowded. By today's teachers' union standards we probably had about three and half classes' worth of students in that room all being taught by a very old looking nun. I remember thinking, or hearing someone else say, that she looked like she could be teaching us the story of the Crucifixion from personal memory. From the eyes and intellect of a six-year old boy, it seemed they could have been right. Her name was Sister Anna Willetta, and I will never forget her name or her face.

I have a clear recollection of my very first embarrassing moment in elementary school that took place in that first grade classroom. Sister Anna Willetta was trying to put together a little Christmas show for the parents and was scouting out who had "talent" – who could sing, who could dance, etc. Since I hadn't been selected in the singing and dancing category, I tried to squeak in by way of the etc. division. I remember not wanting her to think I was talentless, but not sure that I wanted everyone to know what my talent was, so I approached the nun and in a very low voice told her I could wiggle my ears. Ruthlessly, she repeated what I had said in a voice loud enough for all to hear, and then had me perform a demonstration for the class. I felt like a personification of Dumbo the Elephant, and was thereafter quite selective in who I told about my ear wiggling, and what I told to nuns. I remember being upset about my embarrassment when I got home and comforted myself by indulging in some of Mom's rice pudding. Nobody else made rice pudding like she did. It seemed like every spoon absorbed a little more of the pain.

However, several months later my artistic desires were satisfied when I was selected by Sister Anna Willetta to play the part of Abraham Lincoln in a little skit that we put on to honor his birthday. I remember the plot of the skit was that Lincoln, at a young age, worked as a store clerk and realized after a customer had left that the customer was not given the right change. Honest Abe walked, miles, in the snow, to catch up with the customer to give him back his money. Of course, when I told the family that I was going to play Abe Lincoln, I got ribbed by Rob who walked around the house for the next week with the dishtowel draped around his chin like a beard.

When first grade ended I had my first experience of "summer vacation" from school. Mom and Dad were great about always giving Rob and me a real vacation experience at some time during the summer. I can't exactly remember where we went year-by-year, but can tell you that every year we went someplace special, together as a family, by car, and Dad always made it a learning experience. Those places included: Niagara Falls in Canada; Gettysburg, President Eisenhower's retreat and the Amish Country in Pennsylvania; Plymouth Rock, Hyannisport (President Kennedy's retreat), Cape Cod and the cranberry bogs in Massachusetts; Washington, DC; Cooperstown, Saratoga and West Point, in New York; and Annapolis, in Maryland. And there were several summers where Mom and Dad rented a bungalow in upstate New York for a couple of weeks, in places whose names I still remember, like Ellenville, Palenville, Tannersville and Saugerties, and which I can picture clearly. These trips (and the stays at the bungalows) usually took up two weeks of the summer.

One of my favorite places to visit, in fact, probably my favorite, hands down, was Connecticut. While Grandpa Sisto had established his home and family in New York, his younger brother, Alessandro, had settled around New Haven, Connecticut. Uncle Alessandro (known as Uncle Alex throughout the family) had several children, and I came to know and love all of them as aunts and uncles. His son, my Uncle Jimmy, was the closest to my dad, I believe, and he was like another one of Dad's brothers to me. I absolutely adored that man. He had a very special way about him and I find myself, still today, thinking about him and using some of his corny one-liners.

Our family, and I am sure this was not unique to us, used nicknames to distinguish among many family members with the same first name. We had a Small Dominick who when I met him was 65 years old and over 6 feet tall. Aunt Nellie's father's name was Frank, and she and both her sisters married men named Frank, so one got the nickname Flip and the other Hot, and her son, Frank, was called Frankie Junior for years. Cousin Jerry, named after his father, became Poochie, and cousin Jim, because of the number of Jims already in the family, became known as Jimmy Boy. Likewise, my Uncle Jim from Connecticut became known as Jimmy New Haven, to distinguish him from my dad.

The weekend trips to see Aunt Evelyn and Uncle Jimmy, and the rest of the Connecticut branch of the Sabellico family in and around New Haven were always very special. He lived in Woodbridge, a suburb of New Haven, and he was like the unofficial mayor of Woodbridge. He knew everybody and every visit created lifelong memories, from eating wild mushrooms to going to the Yale-Harvard game in the Yale Bowl.

Other than the trips we took, we spent the rest of the summer with our friends playing street games (see Chapter 19) or going to work with Dad to one of the New York City Health Department clinics where he worked (the dark room was always fun), which then meant a fun stop afterwards at some place like Rockaway Beach or Coney Island.

It was in the summer of 1960 that New York City got a new amusement park: Freedomland USA, which was located in Baychester in the Bronx where Co-op City is now. It was a United States history themed park, shaped like the United States, with special attractions for various areas of the country including areas dedicated to Old New York, the Great Chicago Fire, the Pacific Northwest, Lewis and Clark, and the San Francisco earthquake. The Great Chicago Fire was recreated every half hour and at every "show" a group of lucky kids was selected to help man the pump on the fire truck. I definitely remember there was a "live" street show gunfight which was the highlight for the kids every time we went, while the Schaefer Brewery Pavilion was the highlight for the dads.

Freedomland didn't survive past 1964, maybe because the World's Fair opened that year, but while it was open it provided several days of fun and memories for me. Freedomland, covering 205 acres, boasted that it was "The World's Largest Outdoor Family Entertainment Center." Walt Disney World now totals 30,080 acres, over 146 times the size that Freedomland was. But we didn't know about Walt Disney World back then, and we were thrilled with Freedomland.

MOMMA ROSA'S RICE PUDDING CUSTARD

This is the rice pudding I grew up with, not the soft, creamy kind you get at the diner. This rice pudding was one of my mom's favorite desserts, and I remember her and my grandmother making it this way. It is really custard baked with rice and raisins, which I am sure you could leave out, if raisins are not one of your favorite things. Mom had a special glass dish with designs cut into it, which she always used for her rice pudding. The smell of the custard baking with the cinnamon in it filled the house. Sometimes Mom would take a piece while it was still warm from the oven, let it set for a little while, and then top it with cold whipped cream. Then the tray would find its way into the refrigerator and would disappear square by delicious square.

4 eggs
3 cups milk
½ cup granulated sugar
2 teaspoons vanilla extract
2 cups cooked rice
½ to 1 teaspoon cinnamon, depending on taste
1/3 cup raisins, optional

Whisk eggs into a medium saucepan, stir in milk, sugar, vanilla and cinnamon. Heat until hot, but not boiling. Take off heat, stir in rice and raisins, and pour into a lightly greased casserole dish and place the casserole dish in a baking pan with water covering up to one half of the side of the casserole dish. Sprinkle the top with cinnamon. Bake at 325 degrees for an hour to an hour and a quarter, until top is golden brown, stirring once after 30 minutes. Let the custard set before cutting. Top with whipped cream, or fresh fruit, particularly strawberries.

AUNT EVELYN'S WHISKEY CAKE

One of my favorite places to visit was New Haven, Connecticut, where my Dad's cousin, Jimmy, lived with his wife, Evelyn, and their kids, Alex (Rob's age) and Linda (my age). Uncle Jimmy and Aunt Ev were two of my favorite people. I thought it was funny that they actually attached "New Haven" to Uncle Jimmy's name, calling him Jimmy New Haven, so the family could distinguish him from my dad. The really funny thing is that his real name, like my dad's, was Vincent. But for some reason a lot of the Italian guys named Vincent became Jimmy. Uncle Jimmy New Haven was my favorite guy in the whole world. He always made me feel special, as did Aunt Ev. Mom first got this recipe from Aunt Evelyn and since then this cake has made it up and down the Eastern seaboard. Mom loved the recipe and used to bring these cakes to her boss at his summer home in New Jersey, and his home in Hollywood, Florida when she went to visit. After Mom passed away, Dad would continue to make Whiskey Cake. He would invent different varieties by changing the liquor that he used. Sometimes it was a Scotch Cake, or a Drambuie Cake, or a Southern Comfort Cake. Also he would make the batter and bake it in giant muffin tins instead of a Bundt pan, and then freeze the muffins. That enabled him to have a personal size Whiskey Cake when he wanted it. Paula always leaves the walnuts out when she makes this recipe. So, be creative and find the version of this recipe that you like the best. It is pretty simple to make, and it is delicious.

1 package Yellow cake mix
1 package Vanilla instant pudding
5 eggs
¾ cup vegetable oil
½ cup whiskey

½ cup sour cream
1 teaspoon Vanilla extract
½ cup chocolate chips
½ cup chopped walnuts

Combine all ingredients except for chocolate chips and walnuts. Mix with electric mixer until smooth. Fold in chips and walnuts. Pour into greased and floured Bundt pan. Bake at 350° for one hour. Dust with powdered sugar. I especially enjoy this cake when it is fresh out of the oven. It does wonders for a cup of coffee.

CHAPTER 9

UNCLE FRANKIE'S NASH

By August of 1960, we were already living in Grandma Millie and Grandpa Mike's house. It was a four-family apartment building. We lived on the first floor front; my mother's brother, Uncle Mike, lived on the first floor rear, and my grandparents lived upstairs in the rear apartment. The front apartment on the second floor was occupied by the Panzeca family: Anthony and Naomi. I remember she was a nurse and everybody was very impressed with that. Back then most mothers were stay-at-home moms, or secretaries, like my mom, or seamstresses.

The alleyway, which is Brooklynese for the driveway, led to the garage, and passed right by the windows of our apartment. This worked out well when Grandpa Mike, the butcher, would stop under the kitchen window on his way home from work on Thursday nights and hand up a package of meat. Usually it was ground beef and steak, maybe pork chops, and on special occasions he would say he had "diamonds" in the package, which was his nickname for veal cutlets. Sometimes Grandpa Mike would also bring baked goods, which I found unusual since he worked at a meat market. But Joe, the Polish butcher he worked for, (on Sheffield Avenue), carried a line of baked goods, especially Polish specialties like Cheese Babka and Chrusciki (fried strips of dough dusted with powdered sugar), which was as much fun to say as it was to eat. He would also bring home Boston Crème Pie and jelly donuts which were awesome.

In the summertime all of our apartment windows were open because we did not yet own an air conditioner. That would come a little later, and when we did get an air conditioner, we got only one, which went in my parents' bedroom. On real hot nights, Rob and I would drag our bedding into their room to share the cool air.

One day in August 1960, my father was flushing his car radiator and was going to add Bardahl to his oil. The name of that product has stuck in my mind since I very first heard it. It just sounded so mysterious and otherworldly to me. Uncle Frankie had stopped by and invited my family to a barbeque later that day. Since I was obviously being a pest and getting in my dad's way, everyone suggested that I go home with Uncle Frank and the family would catch up with me later.

I jumped at the chance to get to sit in the front seat of Uncle Frankie's blue Nash. As the youngest in my family of four, I always had to sit in the back seat in Dad's Buick, but riding alone with Uncle Frank got me the front seat. On the way from East New York to Ozone Park, on the corner of Milford Avenue and New Lots Avenue, our ride came to an abrupt end, when a car drove through a stop sign and crashed into us. Untethered by any seat belt, (since Ralph Nader hadn't broken on the scene yet), my young body hurled from the cherished front seat to the unyielding windshield and my head smashed into it. The next thing I remember, I am sitting on the curb with a blood soaked towel over my face and there is a crowd of people and police officers around us.

The police notified my parents and I remember seeing my dad running out of his car toward me. He was wearing a sleeveless, tank top t-shirt and was sweating profusely. He wouldn't wait for an ambulance. He picked me up, carried me to his car and took me to the hospital which was on New Lots Avenue across the street from the Biltmore Theatre. They took an x-ray of my skull, which showed no injuries. I remember my dad trying to make me laugh by telling me about Dizzy Dean, a Hall of Fame baseball pitcher with the Cardinals, Cubs and Browns during the 1930s and 40s, who was x-rayed after being hit in the head and the headlines the next day read: Dean's Head Examined; Nothing Found. Distraction was one of Dad's specialties, and baseball was never far from his mind.

Despite the fact that there were no fractures or internal injuries to my head, there were dozens of tiny shards of glass in my skull, and my face had been cut, just to the side of my nose. I remember them talking about stitches, but seeing that it was in my smile line, they decided to just let it heal. Then an Asian doctor with a long narrow tweezers began picking the shattered glass out of my skull. I was too scared to move a muscle. Luckily for the doctor, he had a clear shot at seeing where the glass was. When we were kids, as soon as school ended every year, our parents took us to Frank the Barber on Shepherd Avenue and we got crew cuts. We were left with very little hair on our scalps (which is the way a lot of men wear it today), and with a tuft of hair in the front, which we stiffened with Butch Wax. Yuch! I guess the idea was that we only needed one haircut all summer, and it kept us cooler.

Uncle Frank's car, the Nash, which everybody called an upside-down bathtub because of its shape, was too damaged to move from the scene of the accident, and, anyhow, Uncle Frank was probably too shaken to drive it. I remember going back to the accident scene the next day with my dad and Uncle Frank, and somebody had poured ketchup on the dented portion of the fender, to make it look like blood. Then my dad showed me the front windshield, which was supposedly "shatter-proof" (whatever that really means) but which was completely smashed to smithereens, and at the center of the shatter marks was a circle the size of my head.

The end result of that accident was a lawsuit brought to compensate me for the scar on my face. It was my introduction to the legal system. I remember being brought into the judge's chambers, to be seen by the judge who had to approve the settlement of the case, which was for about $1,500. The judge made a remark that I should put the money away and it would help me pay for law school one day. As it turns out, the money was held in an account for my benefit until I was 21, and it was used by me toward my law school tuition.

My Second Grade Class, seventy students and 1 nun, Sister M. Francis Martin.

Maria Milza and me on the day we received First Communion.

CHAPTER 10

CATHOLIC SCHOOL – PART II

SECOND GRADE – SISTER FRANCES MARTIN

Having survived the trauma of the first grade, I made it across the hall to Sister Frances Martin and the second grade. The big challenges that year would be to learn how to write in script, to prepare for Holy Communion and to handle the transition from Sister Anna Willetta's pace to that of a nun born in this century. Sister Frances Martin was a young go-getter. There was no nonsense tolerated by her. She wanted everything done in "two shakes of a lamb's tail" (her favorite saying) and done her way.

I remember to this day that she had rules about everything. Rules on how to cover our books (we had to use plain brown paper that we got from turning the grocery bags inside out), rules on how to divide our composition books by folding down pages at certain intervals to divide the subjects, rules that included writing the initials "I.M.D.G." on the top of every paper we wrote on, followed by drawing a cross, although to be honest I had no idea what IMDG stood for. (I have since come to learn that it was an abbreviation for In Majorem Dei Gloriam – To the greater glory of God.) I am sure that as seven year olds, we came up with our own meaning, but I just don't remember. I do remember that I came to learn that the INRI on the top of the crucifix stood for Jesus, King of the Jews, although as kids we joked that it stood for "I'm Nailed Right In" and when we said it we quickly made the sign of the cross for fear that the earth would open up immediately and swallow us whole for our blasphemous humor, or just as severe – a nun might hear us and make us wish we had never been born. The fact that the earth didn't take us in, or a nun didn't punish us, did not diminish our fear that it would happen the next time we were brazen enough to joke in the same vein.

My brother was three years older than I was, but he had not experienced Sister Frances Martin. He had started school in St.

Rita's Parish and I always envisioned St. Rita's as being a more established and easier school, probably because I wasn't going there. It was during the second grade that I thought my Catholic school education, if not my life, was going to be terminated, thanks to Sister Frances Martin, and the other nuns who seemed to get their "jollies" from picking on little kids. We had been arranged to sit in class in the second grade in alphabetical order. My main objection to that was that it separated me from my best friends, Johnny Chisefsky (the single greatest athlete I ever met), and Maria Milza (who was adorable and lived next door to me, and who all the boys had a crush on). Being in school, in uniform, with a white shirt and a tie, was tough enough, but what was I going to do stuck among the Ps, Rs, and Ts. I wanted to be with the cool kids who all happened to have last names that started with letters in the first half of the alphabet. Well, those were the rules, so I had to live with them. As bad as they were for me, there was a girl in my area of the room, which happened to be the back, who could not see the board, despite the thick glasses she wore. The glasses were only one component of her not being considered one of the "pretty" girls, which we had already figured out at age seven. She was extremely shy and not particularly attractive, the former possibly caused by the latter.

One morning, I made fun of that girl, by passing a remark to Joseph R. about how ugly she was, or some other juvenile observation. Sister Frances Martin, with the power of super bionic hearing bestowed upon nuns by God, overheard it, and took the opportunity to make an example out of me.

Back then, we had a break in the school day, and if you lived close enough to the school you got to go home for lunch. We were known as "walkers." The kids who took the bus to school ate their brown bag lunches in the auditorium and got a chance to buy a bag of potato chips for 5 cents and an 8 ounce container of milk for 2 cents, or chocolate milk for 3 cents. Since we lived on the same block as the school, and both my parents worked, my brother and I used to go home to Grandma Millie's apartment for a hot cooked meal. Usually it was some type of homemade soup or stew, or eggs and whatever Grandma had, especially during Lent when we could not eat meat (potatoes and eggs, peppers and eggs, mushrooms and eggs, etc.) My favorite was *mozzarella en carrozza*, which was my grandmother's Italian version of French toast. She dipped Italian bread in beaten eggs and fried it, but first she made a sandwich out of it, with a generous portion of mozzarella cheese as the stuffing. My brother and I would make a contest out of it to see who could get the mozzarella cheese to string out the longest from the sandwich before it broke. Then we would spin the strung out cheese around the sandwich and eat it. Grandma was always ready for us with a great meal and we hated to go back to school.

Just as an aside, besides Grandma Millie's fabulous cooking, the thing I loved her for most was her admonishment to my father in Italian: lascile le (la-sha-lee) - which meant "leave him be" – when Dad's temper had risen and I was about to get spanked. I loved that Italian phrase – lascile le.

Well, on the day I made fun of the girl with the thick glasses, Sister Frances Martin told me that I could not go home for lunch. In fact, my punishment was to stand in the corner of the room while everyone else went to lunch. For one hour I was to stand in the corner of the second grade classroom by myself. My life was over and I knew it. The embarrassment of being singled out by the teacher, being alone in the classroom, missing lunch with my grandmother, were all minimal compared to my greatest fear, which was having to deal with my father when he found out why I didn't come home for lunch that day.

As I stood in the corner I began to cry out loud. I thought about missing lunch. I thought about my brother and grandmother waiting for me. I thought about having to be alone in that room, but mainly I thought about my father and the shaving strop he used to instill punishment. I cried louder. Then the fourth grade nun, Sister Saint Agatha entered the room, causing me to believe she was my savior. She asked me what happened, and through sobbing I told her. She told me I couldn't stay alone and I should go home. I raced down the block, and on the way made up a story as to why I was late, telling my grandmother I had to help the nun clean the blackboards.

After lunch the kids from all eight grades in the school congregated in the schoolyard. We flipped baseball cards, or played ring-a-levio, and generally just ran around for a while until one of the nuns rang the bell, which we responded to like Pavlov's dogs, forming double lines by grade to enter the school. That afternoon, after the bell sounded, and we formed our lines, Sister Frances Martin spotted me and inquired as to my freedom against her direction. I told her I had been sent home by the fourth grade nun. When we got back to our classroom, Sister Frances Martin announced in front of the whole class, that since I listened to the fourth grade nun instead of her I should be in the fourth grade. She sent me to the closet in the back of the room to get my jacket and briefcase, and made me empty my desk into my briefcase, sending me down the hall to the fourth grade. Now I knew I was dead. This was going too far and for sure they were going to tell my dad. Through tears, I packed all my books as the other kids looked at me and giggled, a combined product of laughing at my embarrassment, and nervous laughter that it could have just as easily been them suffering my humiliation. It was going to get worse.

I walked down the hall to the fourth grade and knocked on the door. There I was greeted by my liberator, who I came to learn was really an accomplice in my punishment. She asked me why I was there, and then assigned a desk to me and had me unpack my briefcase. As soon as that was done, she proceeded to teach a lesson in Geography, a subject that was first taught in the fourth grade then. Within minutes of starting the lesson she called on me to answer a question. Obviously, I did not know the answer. She immediately told me that if I didn't know the answer then I didn't belong in the fourth grade, and I should get my jacket, pack up all my books and go back to the second grade. Now I was being laughed at by fourth graders. I complied with her direction and walked back down the hall to my original classroom. There, Sister Frances Martin took me back in after dishing out another reprimand about my conduct. The final act of this drama was played out on my rear end, because it was just not acceptable then for parents to hear from the nuns that their child misbehaved.

Truth be told, I never really got a good grade for conduct in elementary school. Many a day I would have to stay after class to erase the blackboards because I had talked in class. I used to tell Dad that the nuns asked me to erase the boards because I was one of the taller kids. I would get report cards with 99s and 100s in my subjects but only S (Satisfactory) for Conduct, and sometimes even a U (Unacceptable). Those were hard to explain at home, despite the excellent academic grades, and that made it hard to sit down for a few days. Getting report cards in Catholic school was a production. The nuns didn't just hand them out. We received a visit from either the principal or the pastor who had the honor of distributing the report cards to us. Knowing that we were going to receive a special visitor we rehearsed a special song which we performed when they arrived. I specifically remember singing *Climb Every Mountain* (from *The Sound of Music*), and *Getting To Know You* (from *The King and I*) when Father Tully visited us for the first time after replacing Monsignor Cavanaugh.

Despite the traumatic episode of being yo-yoed from the second grade to the fourth grade, second grade wasn't a total bad memory. Three pretty big events happened during that school year that were positive: the election of John F. Kennedy, Alan Shepard becoming the first American in space, and my First Holy Communion.

I remember the buzz created by John F. Kennedy running for President. It was the first time I heard about Al Smith, who was the only other Roman Catholic to ever run for President. Everyone in the parish was excited about the prospect of a Catholic becoming the leader of the free world (not that there was any sign that we were being oppressed under President Eisenhower or his predecessors), and when he was elected it was the Catholic equivalent of Jackie Robinson breaking the color barrier of Major League Baseball with the Brooklyn Dodgers.

After Kennedy was elected the National Aeronautics and Space Administration (NASA) space project was a featured program of his administration. Up to that point, as kids in Brooklyn, all we knew about space was very, very little. The moon was made of green cheese, and had an image of Jackie Gleason smiling from it when it was full, and every so often it was "blue." Other than that, we had Flash Gordon episodes to fill our imagination as to what existed and transpired in outer space.

By May 1961, the US was already falling behind the Russians, who had propelled Yuri Gagarin into space on April 12, 1961, making him the first person to do so, beating the Americans who had to scrub their proposed similar mission a few times for technical difficulties. By May the Americans were ready to draw even. I remember Sister Frances Martin wheeling a TV set into the classroom that morning and we were told that something very special was about to happen. There was live television coverage from Cape Canaveral, and I remember being so impressed with the whole telecast, and even the name "Cape Canaveral" seemed so powerful to me! We all sat at attention as the countdown numbers on the screen ticked off and I clearly remember the voice of Mission Control saying "T minus 10 seconds and counting" etc. and then "Blastoff."

The whole class clapped as the rocket took off and we followed its flight on a trajectory chart from Mission Control, which was elementary in retrospect, but looked so advanced then. About fifteen minutes later, the capsule of Freedom 7 splashed down and Alan Shepard had safely returned to earth and we all clapped again. The US was back in the space race.

When you reach the age of seven, it is the time in a young Catholic's life that you get to receive your First Holy Communion. Boy, was that a big deal in Brooklyn in the '50s and '60s. The preparatory process was only a few months, but it seemed like it took forever, since when you are only seven years old a few months is a good portion of your living experience. It was drilled into my head, and the heads of my fellow communicants, that we were about to receive the body and blood of Jesus Christ. That in itself was a bit heavy to lay on a seven year old.

But then the nuns added the news that before we got to receive the body and blood of Christ our souls had to be pure and the only way for that to happen was to receive the sacrament of Penance (go to Confession) and confess all of our sins to a priest. Receiving the sacrament of Penance entailed memorizing the Act of Contrition, which looking back on it, I don't know how contrite we really were when we were reciting something we memorized instead of something from our hearts, and I don't really think any of us knew what "contrition" meant anyway. And the memorization wasn't the worst part. The actual sacrament took place in a dark closet-type structure (a confessional), where a priest sat in a small area and you knelt in a similar size area and the two of you were separated by a screen, with a sliding door. There was also someone on the other side of the priest, and when he was talking to that person you were not supposed to be able to hear their confession. That was the theory anyway.

The nuns taught us the difference between venial sins (the Church's version of white lies) and mortal sins (which could cause you to burn in hell for perpetuity). Times may be a little different now, and maybe kids are more advanced, or precocious, but really how many sins could you have committed before you were seven years old? Knowing that we were at a loss as to what to say the nuns provided us with all the things we did wrong: we lied, we didn't listen to our parents, we didn't wash behind our ears, etc. It was one of the first official installations of guilt made in our minds by our religious leaders.

When you finally got to go to Confession, the priest gave you penance to complete for the absolution of sin he conveyed upon you. The penance was usually a combination of prayers, with a larger number of prayers and a larger number of Our Fathers being dispensed the graver your sins were. Lesser penances consisted of a small number of Hail Marys and Glory Be's. Human nature being what it is we all watched our classmates to see how long they had to pray after their Confession, so we could determine who the "bad guys" were.

Once we got past Confession, the day of Holy Communion was a big event! The boys all wore navy blue suits, with white shirts and white ties and a white carnation in our lapel. The girls all wore miniature bridal gowns, complete with veils. As students of the school, we always attended 9:15 mass on Sunday mornings, but on Holy Communion Sunday there was a special Mass, which included a procession of the communicants. After Mass, the flashbulbs were popping all over the place, as the communicants became the target of their respective family paparazzi. One of the treasured pictures of my childhood shows the beautiful Maria Milza and I standing together like a junior bride and groom in our Communion outfits in the St. Gabriel schoolyard. (That same year, Johnny Mathis recorded the song "Maria" from *West Side Story*. It was the most popular song of the year, and of course, every time I heard it, I thought they wrote it and recorded just for my Maria. *"Maria, the most beautiful sound I ever heard."*)

After all of the picture taking, we all went home to our respective apartment houses and each of our backyards was filled with music, food, wine, and relatives. Were they all so happy that we confessed our sins, that we received the body and blood of Christ, or that it was another occasion for the family to eat, drink and be merry?

THIRD GRADE – MISS LAURO – MY REDHEADED TEACHER

When it came time for me to enter the third grade, in September 1961, the Catholic Church was already having a hard time filling the vocations. I did my part by becoming an altar boy, but that had no effect on the shortage of parish priests and nuns. The immediate impact of the shortage was felt when a letter was sent home that summer to the parents of third graders that their children would be taught by a lay teacher, Miss Emily Lauro. I had never heard the words "lay teacher" before, and at the age of seven, I really didn't know what they meant, but ever since that September whenever I hear those words my mind shows me a picture of a beautiful young woman with flowing red hair and a freckled smiling face. Yes, it was in the third grade that I had my first crush. Precocious little toddler, wasn't I?

Every Christmas my mom would make some special gift for my teachers. I could not possibly tell you what any one of those teachers received from me, or my mom, as a gift, except for Miss Lauro. Starting sometime in October, Mom began to knit a mint green sweater for Miss Lauro. Every day I checked on the status of that sweater. I dutifully fulfilled the job of every boy whose mother knitted back then – spreading my arms apart at shoulder's distance, allowing her to unwind the wool from the skein onto my arms, so that it flowed properly for knitting. I couldn't wait for Mom to finish. I was filled with anticipation and delight to wrap that gift, and to have Miss Lauro unwrap it. I knew that she could not possibly have ever received a present from any student as wonderful as a hand knit mint green sweater. On the last day of school before Christmas, I must have busted the buttons on my school shirt with pride as I handed that festive gift box to Miss Lauro. It is a scene I have played over and over and over.

As for becoming an altar boy, it was held out to Catholic school boys when we reached the third grade that to serve as an altar boy was the highest honor. At that time, which was prior to the Second Vatican Council, the Mass was all in Latin, and if you memorized the prayers and could pass a simple test, you were given the great privilege of becoming an altar boy. Girls were not allowed to serve. We were given the feeling, in that male dominated society, that being an altar boy was a stepping stone to becoming a priest, and girls couldn't do that either. Men were doctors, women were nurses. Men were lawyers, women were secretaries. Men were priests, women were nuns. Brooklyn 1960s.

Rob had already been an altar boy for three years, and it was just a natural assumption that I would follow. As part of my training I memorized the Confiteor:

> Confiteor Deo omnipotenti, beatæ Mariæ semper Virgini, beato Michaeli Archangelo, beato Ioanni Baptistæ, sanctis Apostolis Petro et Paulo, omnibus Sanctis, et tibi, pater: quia peccavi nimis cogitatione, verbo et opere: mea culpa, mea culpa, mea maxima culpa. Ideo precor beatam Mariam semper Virginem, beatum Michaelem Archangelum, beatum Ioannem Baptistam, sanctos Apostolos Petrum et Paulum, omnes Sanctos, et te, pater, orare pro me ad Dominum Deum nostrum.

What I really memorized were syllables. All I really knew was that it was a prayer that altar boys said while kneeling and leaning forward so far that it appeared they were speaking directly to the altar floor, and that when they said "mea culpa, mea culpa, mea maxima culpa" they would beat their chests, three times, like King Kong did. To be honest, I memorized it, and after becoming an altar boy I recited it hundreds of times, but I never knew what I was actually saying. And after a few years, we would lean forward, and after getting past "Confiteor Deo omnipotenti" most of us would mumble a few Latin phrases, beat our chests three times, and then mumble a few more phrases before getting up. It was the same way with many of the other prayers. I knew that when the priest said: "Dominis vobiscum" I was to reply "Et cum spiritu tuo." We really didn't know that it meant "And may the spirit be with you." We kidded that it was the Pope's phone number: Et cum spiri 220.

Having been accepted as an altar boy, your parents now had to buy you your vestments – a cassock and surplice. The cassock was a black, floor length, long sleeve vestment, with snap buttons along the entire front length of the garment. The surplice was white with a square collar and short sleeves. It was just below waist length and was worn over the surplice. These were garments you cherished and respected. You only put them on in the sacristy of the Church. The day you went with your parents to buy your vestments was a special occasion.

Mass was celebrated three times every weekday morning, at 6:15, 7:00, and 8:00. On a rotating basis, the altar boys got different Sunday masses, and might get assigned to one of the daily masses for the week. Since Rob and I lived right next to the Church and School, it seemed like we got an extra share of the 6:15 Mass, and we were always the first ones called if the assigned altar boys didn't show up.

When you were seven or eight years old, the 6:15 Mass was a scary thing. The Church was cavernous, and, as you can imagine, since it was basically empty, it was kept fairly dark. All of the nuns attended that Mass, daily, and they sat together in the front row. The first time I came out and saw that I felt like I was facing a firing squad. There in one aisle was a Catholic school boy's version of Murderers' Row, and you had nothing and nobody to shield you, except the communion rail, and at one point in the Mass, you would be meeting all of them right there, face to face, and staring into their open mouths as they waited for the priest to place the host on their tongue.

Looking past the first row you knew that there were other people in the Church. Although it was difficult to see them, you could hear them, but you had no chance of distinguishing the noises they were making. Later in the Mass, as they came out of the darkness to receive Communion, you could see that they were all old women, mostly all toothless, and all walking with their rosary beads wrapped around their hands. Even as they approached the Communion rail, they continued to pray the Rosary, out loud, and at the speed they were talking, without teeth to help them annunciate, I could never tell if they were praying in English or Italian. They would stop long enough to receive the host, and would then disappear back into the darkness of the Church, to continue praying the Rosary. Years later when I watched the movie *Field of Dreams*, and saw the ballplayers emerge from the cornfield and then return and disappear into the cornstalks, it was eerily similar to the old women appearing from and disappearing into the darkness of the church, and I felt it must have been the product of Ray Kinsella having had experiences similar to mine.

As the only altar boys in the family, Rob and I were asked to serve at the weddings of several of our cousins. I remember being as proud as can be standing there on the altar when my cousin Libby married Tony, and when cousin Frank married Annette, and my kids get a kick out of seeing me there on the altar when they look at my cousins' wedding pictures.

One of the fun experiences of being an altar boy was the annual outing. All of the altar boys, accompanied by a priest and few parent chaperones, got to go to Coney Island for the day. You would get a pass that would get you on all the rides at Steeplechase Park, and you could play as many pinball or skeeball games in the arcade as you could ply nickels and dimes from your dad. Of course, with Rob and me attending, Dad was one of the chaperones. No way were the two of us getting out of his sight on a trip like that. Thanks to Dad we had been to Coney Island many times as a family, but it was special to be there with so many friends. I have two distinct memories of one specific altar boy trip. The first is that it was the one and only time I went on the famous Parachute Jump. The Parachute Jump (whose frame still stands and can be seen from the Belt Parkway) was a ride first built for the 1939 New York World's Fair and moved to Steeplechase Park in 1941. It was 262 feet high and contained 12 two person seats each attached to a parachute. You got belted in, lifted 262 feet and dropped, slowed only by the parachute with your landing softened only by a platform on springs. I remember sitting next to Rob during the descent thinking I would never seem my mother again. I thought maybe they made all altar boys do this to get us closer to God. It cured me of ever wanting to go on any thrill rides again. The Parachute Jump closed in 1968, sparing other children the harrowing experience but depriving millions of the memory.

My other memory of Coney Island was another of those moments when a layer of the onion skin protecting your childhood innocence and naïveté gets peeled away. Having been to Coney Island with Dad several times meant we were very familiar with the famous Nathan's there, where they served hot dogs and thick crinkle-cut French fries, which were known around the world, and novelty dishes like Nathan's Fried Frog Legs and Chow Mein Sandwich. One of the highlights for us was getting an ice-cold draft root beer served directly from the spigot at the bottom of a wooden barrel. We were impressed at this "special" soda. Well, that day they must have been having some technical difficulties, and as we approached the stand, to our horror (bit of a strong word), one of the counterpeople opened the barrel to reveal a set of pipes and hoses, letting on that our special root beer was served just like all the other fountain sodas, just with better marketing.

In February 1962, the United States took its next step in the space program, launching John Glenn into outer space on the Friendship 7 as the first American to orbit the earth. We were again allowed to watch the blastoff on television and followed his path throughout the day. By 3 o'clock that afternoon, Glenn had orbited the earth 3 times, having traveled over 75,000 miles at a speed of over 15,000 miles an hour. Everyone was amazed and proud. Progress and the future were zooming towards us!

MOZZARELLA EN CARROZZA

The mere mention of this dish brings me back to the second floor apartment of my Grandma Millie in Brooklyn. She is at the stove, placing each of the cheese sandwiches into the oil carefully. My brother Rob and I are at the table, waiting anxiously. We are home from school for lunch. Then Grandma places the fried sandwiches on our plate, and as soon as they are cool enough to touch, we each pick one up, take a bite, and string out the melted mozzarella as far as it will reach before it snaps, then we whip the sandwich around, causing the melted mozzarella to wrap around it. We laugh, as only kids can laugh, and we polish off our lunch, and then head back to the St. Gabriel's schoolyard, happy and content.

8 slices of bread (bread should be about 2-3 inches in diameter
¾ cup milk
4 eggs, beaten
Breadcrumbs
Flour
1 pound mozzarella cheese

Oil

Moisten the bread with a small amount of milk. Cut mozzarella into slices the same thickness as the bread. Insert a slice of mozzarella between two slices of bread. Coat with flour, dip in beaten eggs, then coat with breadcrumbs and fry in a skillet with fairly deep, hot oil. Repeat the process until all the bread and cheese have been used.

As an appetizer you can serve this dish with some heated marinara sauce, or can get creative by adding anchovy fillets inside the sandwiches and serve with lemon slices. But, back in Brooklyn, for lunch, we had them just as they were, fresh out of the skillet.

CHAPTER 11

CAMP

Every so often the nuns would send us home with information on this or that society or organization. My memory is that my parents, or at least my dad, were not real big "joiners." Dad coached the St. Gabriel baseball team that my brother was on, the Cubs, and I was the bat boy, and I remember that he was really involved in the baseball program in general. I also remember him being in the Holy Name Society, and once a year we attended an event called a Communion Breakfast. All the members of the society, all male, attended the same Mass, received Communion, and then traveled to a local restaurant for a breakfast. Other than that we were pretty much into family and not outside organizations, although there were so many of my family members living within walking distance of my house, that being involved in my family WAS being involved in my community.

The first three years I attended St. Gabriel's, somewhere about March or April of each year, the nuns had sent me home with a flyer for the CYO Summer Day Camp, held at Clearview/Whitestone, in the shadow of the Whitestone Bridge, literally. The thought of summer camp appealed to me. They made it sound, and look, great; pictures of kids having a great time, smiling, laughing, and having fun. I nagged my parents to let me go. They didn't buy into it. There was no way that at age 7 or 8 I was being allowed out of their sight, on a bus, in rowboats, swimming, etc. I would only come to understand many years later that their nerves, and especially my dad's, would not have been able to handle it. It is funny how much becomes apparent to you when you become a parent. Besides, I had my grandparents there to watch me all summer, and my friends on the block, my parents reasoned. They told me about all the "fun" I would miss on Essex Street if I was off at some camp. Reluctantly or otherwise, I lived with it.

Then, in the fourth grade there it came again: that same white, tri-fold brochure, with the same kids, still having a great time, smiling, laughing, and having fun, as if to taunt me that I didn't join them last summer. For whatever reason, which could have been Grandma getting a little older, or my persistence, my parents relented and agreed to let me attend the camp for two weeks, which was one "session." The reason may have been that Johnny Chisefsky also pressured his parents, who said "Yes." That created a period of excitement. I looked forward to my first camp experience with unbridled anticipation. I would be escaping from the asphalt and concrete playgrounds and would be spending a summer camping: morning hikes through wooded parks, outdoor barbeques, afternoons by the pool, and boat rides under the Whitestone Bridge.

As the big day drew closer, the realization set in that I would be taking a school bus to the camp. I had never been on a school bus. I lived so close to my school that if I left my house and directly entered the back door of a bus and got out the front door of the bus I would be at the school. At first the thought of the bus ride seemed exciting too, until the first day. Then those axiomatic words of my mother began to ring out: be careful what you wish for, you might get it. The bus left from the school, and as I boarded there were only a few kids on the bus. Other than John Chisefsky, I didn't know any of them. But the empty seats and my shyness allowed me to get a window seat and sit with John by ourselves. That was the good news, and that was all the good news. The fact that the bus was pretty empty was a sign that we had many stops to make before we got to the camp. My ride to camp began with a one hour bus tour of parts of Brooklyn and Queens I had never seen before, and I didn't get to see much of them the first couple of days on the bus either, because my head was down in my lap, as I tried to fight off a serious case of nausea. The next few mornings Mom sent me off to the bus stop with Juicy Fruit Gum, with the thought that the sugar would help calm my stomach. After a few days my stomach calmed down, either because of the gum, or because I had become familiar with the scene. Anyway, by the third day, I knew all the words to *Michael, Row the Boat*

Ashore, which was sung on the bus every morning and every afternoon, more than once. The song was hugely popular then based on a version recorded by The Highwaymen and by Harry Belafonte. The irony lost on us young campers was that it was a song sung by black slaves in the Georgia Sea Islands as far back as 1863. It was a rowing song sung on their way to work. Many believe that the Michael referred to was the Archangel Michael. There was also a much simpler, less reverent, song that the camp veterans taught to us rookies: I don't want to go to CYO; Gee, Mom, I want to go home.

I forgot all about the bus trip when the counselor brought our group into the changing room to prepare to go swimming. As we entered the chlorine-laden air of the locker room, I stopped dead in my tracks, surrounded by the sight of what I remember as over a hundred boys all in various stages of nudity – getting into or out of their swimming trunks. My brother and I never even bathed together. Nothing in the brochure prepared me for that scene. After we got into our suits we had to put on rubber bathing caps which identified our swimming skill: red for beginners, blue for medium, and white for advanced swimmers.

Eventually we got to lunch time. Every group of campers was assigned to a table where we waited for lunch. I didn't know what to expect (although I kind of figured it wouldn't be my grandmother's *mozzarella en carrozza*) and I didn't know what to do when presented with the camp's version of lunch – a bologna sandwich on white bread with butter spread on each slice of bread. White bread? Butter on bologna? Could things get any weirder? The answer was yes. They told us that our beverage for lunch was something called "bug juice." Looking back on it, I think it was nothing more than Kool-Aid, but I'm still not convinced that the little flecks floating in it were not really bugs.

At the end of the first week, we were told that in the second week we were going on a special trip for a "cookout." We were instructed to each bring in two hot dogs wrapped in aluminum foil, which everybody in Brooklyn called "tin foil." Mom wrapped up the hot dogs and off to camp I went, all excited about the cookout. When we got to camp we were brought to another bus which brought us to Alley Pond Park in Douglaston, Queens, about five miles from the camp. After hiking throughout the Park, to tire us out I guess, we were brought to an area with grills, where the counselors cooked our hot dogs and gave them back to us on buns. Then we had to "hunt" for sticks to roast marshmallows.

Mom and Dad signed me up for a two week session at the camp. During two of the ten days it poured, which spared me from the locker room scene. In its place, we did Arts and Crafts all morning, which consisted of making a comb holder from two strips of leather and a piece of lanyard, and in the afternoon we were bussed to an auditorium where they showed cartoons. On one of the sunny days they made all of us strap on lifejackets (a new experience for me), loaded us all on boats (The King, The Queen or The Manhattan) and said we were going rowing under the Whitestone Bridge. Looking back, I really don't think that our "rowing" had anything to do with powering the boats. All I could think about at the time was how pissed my father would be if something happened to us on that boat.

That summer Allan Sherman released his hit single, "Hello Muddah, Hello Fadduh (A Letter from Camp)" and I swore he was writing about my experiences.

Grandma Sabellico with Dad in his Victory Garden.

CHAPTER 12

DAD'S VICTORY GARDEN

Although I have distinct memories of the bug juice and other assorted thrills of summer camp and summer on the streets of East New York, the thing that really identifies Brooklyn summers in my mind is Dad's garden. It created a pastime for him and the family from spring through fall. Together with Grandpa Mike's Thursday night packages, it also provided much of the menu for a good portion of the year. And the fruits, vegetables and flowers he grew were a source of true pride for Dad.

As part of the country's war effort during World War II, the government rationed food, and there were shortages of labor and gasoline, which impacted the trucking of whatever produce was available. Partly because of those reasons, and, I think, as a way to boost morale, the government urged civilians to plant "Victory Gardens." The idea took root, so to speak, and the records show that almost 20 million Americans started growing their own fruits and vegetables. As soon as Dad got out of the Navy he was one of the 20 million, and in the 1950s, in the chronological shadow of World War II, in Brooklyn, home vegetable patches were still called "Victory Gardens."

Dad was an avid gardener and made the whole family part of it. I have very strong memories of the gardens he would grow in Brooklyn, and then in Massapequa after that. Luckily, both of the houses we lived in on Essex Street had empty lots next to them, and Dad quickly commandeered them for his gardens. He would lay out a design that included beautiful flowers nearest to the street for people to enjoy as they passed by. He was especially proud of the roses, gladiola, and poppies. He would grow them in all colors and we all enjoyed the rainbow effect it created. Along the side fence were the string beans and squash. The largest part of the garden consisted of neat rows of peppers, eggplants, tomatoes, and lettuce. There was always mint and basil. Dad loved his fresh basil (*basilico* in Italian). I can see him clipping off a couple of basil leaves, by hand, tearing them in half, and enjoying the piquant aroma. He just loved to do that. To this day the smell of fresh basil brings me back to my dad's side in his garden.

The first sign that winter was coming to an end was the arrival of the W. Atlee Burpee Seed Catalog in the mail. Rob and I always laughed at the name, picturing the poor guy whose friends must have always made fun of his name – Burpee – and imaging how bad his actual first name must have been if he used an initial and his middle name, Atlee, which we had never heard of. Anyway, when the catalog came, Dad quickly marked out his favorites – the Burpee Big Boy Tomato (a hybrid they had just developed in 1949), and his Gladiola and Poppies, and assorted other seeds and bulbs he needed, to supplement those he had saved from last year's crop. Then Rob and I each got to pick our own vegetable to order. I admit now that I was never very practical about it. I would pick corn because it was tall and different, and I wanted to see the plants grow high, but each stalk only produced one ear and our garden wasn't big enough to grow much corn. Buying products from a catalog in the 1950s was very different from buying products today. You relied on the pictures in the catalog and there was no fax or Internet or FedEx. So Dad would fill out a form, mail it out with a check and we would wait three or four weeks for the seeds and bulbs to come in the mail.

Dad would start his vegetable plants inside, and then transfer them into his own "hothouse" – a contraption he built with three sides and old French doors, (with a lot of window panes) to let in the light and keep out the wind and cold. When the plants got strong enough he transplanted them into their permanent spot in the summer garden.

I can remember being given the honor of filling the old tea pot Dad used as a watering can and watering the plants, when it was deemed I was old enough and responsible enough not to drown them, or step on them. I also remember going out in the early morning and picking the squash flowers, to be cooked up in a pancake type batter. I remember looking through the tomato plants for those caterpillars that had a tremendous ability to camouflage themselves, and they were the enemy because they would eat the leaves and, more importantly, the tomatoes. Dad hated them so much that I remember he let us kill those buggers however we wanted to. I remember picking the tomatoes and leaving the slightly less than ripe ones on a board in the sun for a day or two. And I remember the baseball bat squash (cucuzzi) (pronounced "ga-gootz"), growing on the fence between our lot and Mrs. Fox's house. I was always anxious to pick the fruit and vegetables, and had to be taught the patience to wait for them to ripen. Watching the squash grow and develop into the shape of a baseball bat was always fun for a kid, for me anyway. I remember that toward the end of the summer Dad would let certain flowers, vegetables and fruits "go to seed," and he would put the seeds in envelopes and mark them carefully for the next year, like he was cheating on Burpee a little.

One of the signature elements of Dad's Victory Garden was his fig tree. He was very proud of that tree. He would tell us about how the fig tree had two crops, a spring crop (which wasn't very productive) and a fall crop which could be plentiful. His favorite way to enjoy the figs was right off the tree. He would pick a ripe fig and then split it open and show us the ripe, red, juicy inside before devouring it with a satisfied sigh. The fruit of the fig tree is very delicate, and once ripe must be consumed within a day or it goes bad. We couldn't possibly eat all of the figs that the tree produced, so Mom would make a fig jam which was delicious. She used it as a spread for toast or bagels, and would use it as a filling between layers of a layer cake.

The fig tree brought with it the annual chore of preparing it for the New York winter. As Dad would tell us every year, since the fig tree was native to the Mediterranean and climates like California, it had to be protected from New York's winter climate. Every November, after the fall crop was finished, and the fig tree lost its leaves, we would repeat the tradition of wrapping the tree. First all the branches of the tree were gathered together and tied with twine, so that the whole tree was only about two feet around. Then we would take old newspapers, crumple them up and fill in the spots between all the branches. The next step was to wrap the tree in tar paper or old carpet, and the final step was to put a bucket on top of the tree to stop rain from getting in. Still today, you could drive through any neighborhood, and pick out the Italian families by noticing the tied up fig trees during the winter.

When we were getting ready to move from Brooklyn to Massapequa, Dad was very concerned that we would be able to take the fig tree with us. I guess it was one of his ties to Brooklyn and his family. I remember him asking my cousin, Mickey, if he could move the fig tree and Mickey gladly obliged. Mickey is an ox of a man, and had unbelievable natural strength, matched only by his natural sense of humor. Mickey showed up with his truck ready to move a tree, and when he saw the fig tree he said to my dad, "This isn't a tree, it's a bush!" and with minimum effort he unearthed the family botanical treasure, lifted it onto his truck single-handedly and relocated it to Massapequa. Shoots of that tree made it to my home in Farmingdale, and to this day we enjoy its fruits.

ITALIAN TOMATO SALAD

12 – 15 ripe plum tomatoes, diced
1 small onion, thinly sliced
6 cloves garlic, minced
Basil
Salt
Pepper
Italian seasoning
Olive oil
Balsamic vinegar

NOTE: Generally, this salad tastes much better when it is made about ten to fifteen minutes before serving, and is not refrigerated prior to serving.

Start by dicing the tomatoes into ½ inch pieces, and place in a large bowl; add sliced onion and minced garlic;

The best basil to use is fresh from the garden, clip several leaves, wash them under cold water and tear the leaves into the salad – use at least five or six good-sized leaves; if fresh basil is not available you can use dried basil, but a better alternative is for you to freeze leaves of basil when it is in season: take the leaves, wash them, pat them dry with paper towel and freeze in a Tupperware container, for use as needed.

Add a pinch of pepper and Italian seasoning, and a generous pinch of salt.

Add enough olive oil so that the tomatoes are coated, but not "swimming" in the oil; add balsamic vinegar one teaspoon at a time, until the salad is good to your taste. Be careful not to add too much vinegar at once, it is a very strong ingredient and can quickly overpower the salad.

Serve with plenty of Italian twist bread.

NOTE: My mom made this salad without vinegar. It is a matter of taste.

MOM'S SQUASH FLOWERS
FIORI DI ZUCCA

Dad was the gardener in the family, and was a pretty good cook, truth be told. But some dishes were just Mom's domain and specialty, like her rice pudding, and ice box cakes, Christmas cookies, and other delights. Another of Mom's specialties, which was enjoyed during the summer, were squash flowers, which Mom cooked like fritters. The flowers are both male and female. The female flowers grow on the end of the zucchini "fruit" and are not to be picked. That would get Dad pretty hot. The male flowers, somewhat smaller, are the flowers used for this recipe. This is a very versatile dish. It could be breakfast, lunch, part of dinner, or sometimes just a snack as we sat outside and Dad showed us the constellations in the evening sky, including Orion's Belt, the Little Dipper, and the Big Dipper.

1 dozen large squash flowers (blossoms)
½ teaspoon salt
1 cup flour
1 teaspoon olive oil
¾ cup cold water or seltzer
2 eggs
Oil for frying

Remove most of the stem from each flower. You must handle the flowers gently at every stage or they will rip since they are very delicate. Open flowers and remove the pistils by pinching them at their base. Rinse the flowers in cold water, drain, then spread out on a cloth or paper towel, and leave aside until most of the moisture has been absorbed.

Sift flour and salt into a bowl, make a well in the center and add oil and most of the water. Gradually stir flour into the liquid, adding the balance of the water and the eggs.

Heat oil until a bit of batter dropped into it will sizzle. Dip flowers into the batter and fry a few at a time until they are golden brown all over. Drain on paper towel and serve hot.

Sometimes Mom would add a little sugar to the recipe and it would be more like a pancake batter. As a dessert item she might sprinkle the finished fritters with powdered sugar.

POP'S "BASEBALL BAT"
SQUASH & CHOPPED MEAT

Few recipes have the ability to bring me back to summer and my dad like this one. My son Chris describes this dish as "summer in a spoon." This recipe was one that Dad would make quite often. It featured those baseball bat squash ("cucuzzi") and chopped meat (we didn't call it "ground beef" back in Brooklyn.) In fact, for variety, you could use pork or veal, but we usually used beef. Chris has made this dish with ground turkey and it was delicious. It makes a great sauce to be served over pasta. My favorite is Rigatoni. Enjoy.

2 large "baseball bat" squash, peeled and cubed (about 8 to 10 cups)
2 onions, sliced thin
6 cloves of garlic, diced
2 lbs. of chopped beef
2 large cans crushed tomatoes
A few pinches of sugar
Olive oil
Salt
Pepper
Crushed red pepper, to taste
Italian seasoning
Several leaves of fresh basil

Peel and cube the squash and remove the seeds. Place the cubed squash in a bowl.

Slice the onion and dice the garlic. In a sauce pot, heat several teaspoons of olive oil; add onion, garlic, crushed red pepper, salt and pepper. After a few minutes, when onion starts to get soft and translucent, add ground beef and cook until beef is browned. Add Italian seasoning. Open cans of tomato and add a pinch of sugar to each can. Add crushed tomatoes to pot, stir well. Then add squash. Bring the mixture to a simmer and cover. Cook for approximately one hour, or until the squash is tender.

Boil pasta, cook al dente.

While the pasta is boiling, add a few leaves of fresh basil to the sauce, letting it cook only a minute or two. Serve squash mixture over pasta. We always used a good amount of grated cheese on this dish. It is a distinctive summer dish that made the summer special.

CUCUZZA AND POTATOES

Cucuzza, the long baseball-bat shaped squash, is a funny kind of commodity. They grew on vines that climbed up the fences and could take over the garden if you let them. They also had these white flowers that only opened at dusk, to allow pollination by hawk moths during the night. Some summers the cucuzzi are hard to find, or grow, and some summers you just have an abundance of them. It reminds me of Ogden Nash's little poem about Christmas Mail: *Christmas mail is like a ketchup bottle; None will come and then a lot'll.* Anyway, during those summers when the bat squash is plentiful you need to have a second recipe or you will get bored of eating it the same way. I suggest this recipe, either as a side dish with a barbequed steak, or over pasta.

2 large "baseball bat" squash, peeled and cubed (about 8 to 10 cups)
6 potatoes, peeled and cubed
Olive oil
3-4 cloves garlic, diced
Salt
Pepper
Italian seasoning
Olive oil
Crushed red pepper

Peel and cube the squash and remove the seeds. Pour about ¼ cup olive oil into a pot; add garlic and a light sprinkle of crushed red pepper flakes. When the garlic is lightly browned, add the squash and potatoes, (you can also several crushed tomatoes at this time if you like, preferably fresh) stir until the vegetables have been coated with the olive oil. Lower the heat; add enough water (or chicken stock) so that the vegetables can steam. (As an option you can add a can of crushed tomatoes at this point, if you like.) Cover and let simmer for approximately 30 minutes.

Remove the pot from the stove. Drain 95% of the liquid from the pat. Add olive oil, salt, pepper and Italian seasoning. Return the pot to the stove and cook an additional five to six minutes.

You can serve this dish over pasta or eat as a vegetable. Either way I like to add grated cheese.

ZUCCHINI QUICHE

One of the most prolific producers in the Victory Garden was the zucchini. In a good year, zucchini was abundant throughout the summer. One delicious dish that became a staple at all our summer barbeques was a Zucchini Quiche. It makes me a laugh a little when a say "our summer barbeques." The barbeques at the non-Italian households were hot dogs and burgers, with a side of potato salad. We used the term "barbeque" loosely, because it just wasn't a meal unless it included one or more dishes from the kitchen, and the meat on the grill included sausage, steak and usually an Italian specialty called "fegatelli." Fegatelli are pieces of liver, either pork or veal, wrapped in caul fat (a lacy membrane), with a piece of bay leaf (and sometimes orange slices) tucked in. I know that doesn't sound too appetizing, but trust me, these are delicious. Anyway, back to the Zucchini Quiche. It is a pretty easy, quick recipe that makes a great side dish. Some people prefer to eat it warm, right out of the oven, but it also makes a great treat cold, out of the fridge.

3 cups thinly sliced peeled zucchini (2 large or 4 small)
1 cup Bisquick mix
½ lb mozzarella, diced
½ cup of grated parmesan or romano cheese
4 eggs, beaten
½ cup vegetable oil

Sometimes for variety I will add a little cheddar or provolone cheese.

Preheat oven to 325 degrees. Grease bottom and sides of a 9 inch pie plate.

Stir all ingredients together and pour into pie plate.

Bake for approximately 50-55 minutes until golden brown.

STUFFED ZUCCHINI

The abundance of zucchini led to creativity in the kitchen, and its shape lent itself to being stuffed, once the flesh was scooped out. The majority of time we ate stuffed vegetables (usually peppers or cabbage), the stuffing was a meat and rice mixture. I don't know who came up with this recipe, but it was very popular in our house, especially on Fridays during the summer, when you could not eat meat.

5 zucchini, approximately 8 inches in length and 1 ½ inches in diameter
3 cans tuna fish in water or oil
½ cup bread crumbs
3 stalks celery, diced
2 small onion, diced
2 cloves garlic, minced
2 eggs
Salt
Pepper
Italian seasoning
½ cup grated Parmesan or Romano cheese
Olive oil
8 oz. tomato sauce

Preheat oven to 400 degrees.

Wipe the zucchini with a clean cloth. Cut off the stems and slice the zucchini in half lengthwise, without peeling them. Using a teaspoon or demitasse spoon, scoop out the flesh of the zucchini and place it in a medium sized bowl. After all of the flesh has been removed, place it on a cutting board, chop it coarsely and return it to the bowl.

Place onion, garlic, celery, salt, pepper, and a splash of olive oil in a frying pan and sauté for several minutes. (In today's kitchen you can replace the frying pan by placing these ingredients in a bowl and heating in a microwave for one minute.)

After the onion, celery, garlic mix has cooled; add it to the chopped zucchini flesh. Then add beaten eggs, bread crumbs, and olive oil. The amount of olive oil you add depends on several factors: the size of the eggs, whether you use solid white or chunk light tuna, and whether the tuna is packed in oil or water. Also you are only adding enough bread crumbs to make it a workable stuffing. Too many bread crumbs make the stuffing gummy. You want it to be light and taste more like tuna than bread. Mix thoroughly.

Wipe each of the zucchini halves with a small amount of olive oil, fill in the scooped out portion with a portion of the filling. Fill until the zucchini is rounded. Place the filled zucchini in a roasting pan. Put about a quarter to a third cup of water on the bottom of the pan. You can use chicken broth for extra taste if you are not concerned about eating meat products.

Bake for approximately 15 minutes. Remove zucchini from the oven and spoon tomato sauce on top of the zucchini, enough to cover each zucchini, but not drench them. Continue baking for an additional 30 minutes.

FIG JAM

You could never tell how many figs the tree would produce, and although Dad's favorite way of enjoying the figs was to eat them right off the tree, sometimes the crop was too much to consume. Enter Mom and the fig jam. Since it is difficult to determine how many figs would be available, this recipe is a proportionate one. You really can't determine how much sugar, water or lemon juice to use, until after you have soaked the figs in boiling water, removed the stems, and chopped the figs. Then you would use a half of cup of sugar for every cup of chopped figs.

Fresh ripe figs
Sugar (1/2 cup of sugar for each cup of crushed figs)
Water (3/4 cup of water for each cup of crushed figs)
Lemon juice (1/2 teaspoon for each cup of crushed figs)

Boil four to six quarts of water in a large pot. Once the water has reached a boil, remove it from the heat and place all of the figs in the pot, and soak for ten minutes. The figs will turn a bright green color.

Drain the pot, rinse the figs in cold water and pat them dry. Then cut off all stems, and chop the figs (into about six pieces per fig). Then measure the chopped figs.

Place the chopped figs, sugar, water, and lemon juice into a pot, and bring to a boil. Then reduce the heat and simmer for approximately three hours, stirring every five to ten minutes.

St. Gabriel's RC Church, Linwood Street, Brooklyn, NY.

CHAPTER 13

SUNDAY MORNING

I have come to learn from my Jewish clients and friends that Yom Kippur is the most sacred of days for Jewish people, but that every week's Sabbath observance is just as important, or more important, than all of their other holy days. Similarly, for an Italian Catholic growing up in Brooklyn, Christmas Eve was the holiday which topped the list, but every Sunday we followed rituals which made it clear that Sunday was a day to be reckoned with as a day of importance.

Everything about Sundays in Italian-American Brooklyn was about family, Church, and food, for what would a special day be to Italians without special food? Every one of the four families in the apartment building was Italian, and the ritual was the same for all of them. The Italian-American Sunday morning alarm clock for the rest of the family was the smell of garlic and hot pepper being sautéed in olive oil by Mom, to start the process of making the sauce. While Mom or Grandma Millie was busy starting to create another weekly feast, Rob and I would be off to church, to serve one of several Masses. We never wanted to be assigned to the 7:15 on a Sunday morning; it just didn't seem fair to have to get up and out of the house so early on a Sunday, even before the garlic was browned. The other Mass you didn't want to get assigned to was the 10:15, which was called High Mass, and was con-celebrated, (one of the earliest "fancy" words I learned), which meant that three priests celebrated the Mass. That made for a long time in Church. Anyway, Rob and I would go off to Church to prepare and serve Mass. The Church was within walking distance from the house. In fact, almost everything back then was within walking distance, because that's how we got around.

Mom would "brown" the meatballs, sausage and other meats before putting them in the sauce. Basically, it was searing the outside of the meat to seal in the juices. The risk was that the browned meatballs were very difficult to resist eating, even before they entered the sauce. Uncle Sal was the biggest culprit for "stealing" meatballs.

With the meatballs, sausage and bracciole made and browned, and the sauce started, Mom and Dad would attend the latest Mass we were serving, because we usually served more than one, and after Mass, with the family dressed very respectfully, we would pile into Dad's Buick Century, with the "portholes" in each front quarter panel, which I thought was so cool, and we would head to a bakery for bread and rolls. Sometimes, we would go as far as Atlantic Avenue to Mrs. Maxwell's Bakery, which wasn't an Italian bakery, but had great onion rolls and, on special occasions, Nesselrode Pie or Charlotte Russe.

Safely back at home with our baked treats, we would enjoy a leisurely breakfast. Dad would be reading the Sunday Daily News, New York's Picture Newspaper, especially the sports pages, with the great cartoons by Bill Gallo. Rob and I would steal the comics. I loved reading the funny ones and even followed *Gasoline Alley*, but never quite got into the dramatic, serious ones like *Terry and the Pirates* or the soap opera comics like *Brenda Starr* or *Apartment 3G*. I always read *Dondi*, about the little Italian World War II orphan, who came to America with Uncle Ted, the GI who adopted him and became "Dad." Maybe, I read it because it was on the back cover or because I wanted to be in his Explorers Club, but it was never as much fun as *Dagwood*. After we finished the comics, we would watch Sonny Fox's *Wonderama* on WNEW, which was on every Sunday morning, all morning. Some Sundays we would switch back and forth and watch *Let's Have Fun* with Chuck McCann. There were fewer kids on his show, but it was fun to watch him dress up like the characters in the comics, and you could read along with him, and then he would act out skits with his hand puppets, like Mr. McNasty. Right after his show there was always an Abbott and Costello movie, which we never tired of watching.

All the while, Mom or Grandma Millie was busy assembling a great meal. There was always pasta as a first course. On certain occasions, it would be special pasta, like stuffed shells or manicotti, or lasagna, and on very special occasions, Grandma Millie would make her own ravioli. The mozzarella/ricotta/parmesan mixture in the shells, manicotti, ravioli and lasagna was the same, but somehow each different dish had a unique taste. Since Grandpa Mike was a butcher, the sauce always had great meat in it. I always liked the neck bones. After the pasta came some type of roast meat (beef, chicken or pork), with an assortment of vegetables. Then we finished with ensalada (salad). Dad always said that we ate the salad last because it helped you to digest, and he always told me that restaurants serve it to you first to keep you busy while you are waiting for them to serve you.

After that feast, usually made even more special by the fact that on nine out of ten Sundays there was always company over, the men would usually "retire" to the living room and the comfort of couches, recliners and TV, while the women of the house washed and dried the dishes. Dishwashers were not part of our kitchens in Brooklyn. We only saw them in restaurants. When the dishes were dried and the men worked up a little more appetite (or actually, caught their breath from the first round of eating), Mom or Grandma would ask "Who wants brown and who wants black?", trying to determine how many people wanted "American" (brown) coffee and how many wanted espresso (black), Then they broke out the maganette to brew the black coffee, and would serve it, accompanied by some great baked dessert, and, hopefully, pastry that the company brought. (Holy moley, they brought cannoli!)

MOMMA ROSA'S LASAGNA

When we were kids Mom would let each of us pick our favorite meal for our birthdays, or the Sunday closest to our birthday. My mom continued that tradition even when we were adults, and also did the same for our children. My favorite meal was her lasagna. Each portion was a work of art and love that filled you and satisfied you. To be honest with you, a picture in my mind of my mom preparing and serving her lasagna brings tears to my eyes, and if you know me, you know I am telling the truth. Although everybody puts an emphasis on eating food freshly made, lasagna is one dish that you might consider making ahead of time. If you try to serve it right after taking it out of the oven on the day you make it, the portions get a little sloppy, but if you let it rest and set, the portions cut neatly and the presentation is as pleasant as the taste. Making Mom's lasagna is a several step process, beginning with the tiny meatballs, the sauce, the filling, the noodles, and then the assembly of the dish. As with any recipe, I suggest you read through the entire recipe before you start.

Meatballs:
1 lb. ground beef
1 lb. ground veal
1 lb ground pork
3 eggs
½ cup breadcrumbs
¼ cup fresh parsley, minced
½ cup grated cheese
Salt and pepper, to taste
3 cloves garlic
Pinch of Italian seasoning
Several pieces day-old or frozen Italian bread
½ cup milk

Soak hard or frozen bread in milk, squeeze out milk, and add bread to all other ingredients; mix well; shape into little meatballs, approximately ½" in diameter. Place several meatballs at a time into hot olive oil in frying pan, brown very lightly, just enough to keep them firm. Drain oil and set meat aside.

Prepare a simple marinara sauce, for flavor you can add sausage and meatballs (the larger, "regular" size), or pork and steak, and then remove the meat to serve on a separate platter, or at a different time (good luck with that). For best flavor always use a combination of beef, pork and veal. Pork and veal bones provide excellent flavor, but you must be very careful with the bones. If the sauce is being made just for the lasagna, or for stuffed shells, you may want to add some sliced pepperoni to the sauce. I don't know the exact reason, but the only time Mom added pepperoni to the sauce was when it was being served with a pasta dish that contained ricotta. This was a "trick" she learned from my Aunt Millie, Uncle Louie's wife. (To this day it is a special treat for my family when Cousin Libby (Aunt Millie's daughter) makes Manicotti with tomato sauce with pepperoni on Thanksgiving.)

After the meat has been removed from the sauce, except for the pepperoni, add the meatballs to the sauce and stir, continuing to simmer for approximately one-half hour or so.

Filling:
3 lbs. ricotta cheese
2 lbs. mozzarella cheese, whole milk or part skim, shredded or cubed
½ cup grating cheese
2 eggs
Salt and pepper, to taste
¼ cup fresh parsley, minced

Mix all ingredients well in large mixing bowl, and set aside.

Noodles:
Here you have several options. Mom never used the no-boil type of noodle that is on the market today, and my penchant for custom keeps me from using them, but they are available. The second option, which restaurants use, but Mom didn't, is to use sheets of noodles, which are the same size as the roasting pan. Mom used the lasagna noodles that looked like rulers, and usually used the ones with the curly edges. They always gave the sauce an extra place to hide and were our favorites. Bring the water to boil, place the noodles in the salted water gently, and stir very gently, being careful not to break the noodles. When the noodles were cooked al dente, remove them one at a time and place them over the sides of the scolla pasta, allowing them to drain and to cool a little. Remember not to fully cook the noodle since it will be baking in the oven.

Assembly:
1 lb. mozzarella cheese, sliced
Grating cheese

Set yourself up at a table or counter with a large roasting pan, the pot of sauce with a cupina, the bowl of filling with a wooden spoon, and the noodles. Place enough sauce on the bottom of the pan to fully cover it, then alternate layers of noodles, filling, sauce, noodles, filling, sauce, to fill the pan, finishing with a layer of sauce. Be sure that meatballs and pieces of pepperoni have been distributed generously throughout the layers of sauce.

On top of the last layer of sauce place the slices of mozzarella and then sprinkle with grating cheese. (Optionally, you can garnish with a sprinkle of parsley ot Italian seasoning.) Place the pan in the center of a pre-heated oven and bake at 350 degrees for approximately 40 minutes. When the noodles around the edge start to get a little crispy the lasagna is done. Remove the lasagna from the oven and place the entire pan on a wooden cutting board or cooling rack. As I said before, the lasagna will not slice well when hot.

When the lasagna has set, you can cut it with a pancake flipper. Serve portions that are approximately four inches by four inches, top with a little hot sauce and grating cheese, if desired, and be prepared to be full. From my mom's heart to your kitchen, enjoy!

CHAPTER 14

EASTER

As a kid, I don't know if we actually looked forward to Easter for the fun of Easter, or because it signaled the end of Lent, a period we dreaded. Lent meant sacrifice, something that adults are not very good at, and kids loathe. We were told that we had to give up something for Lent, and you couldn't give up something you didn't like, it had to be something good, like chocolate or soda or pizza or macaroni, God forbid! Also during Lent, every Friday, the nuns would march us down to the Church where we would observe, and participate in, the Stations of the Cross: a 14 step ritual commencing with Jesus being condemned to death and ending with his body being laid in the tomb. And then there were the mite boxes. We were given mite boxes by the nuns at the beginning of Lent, and asked to place coins in them during the Lenten period, and bring them back to class during Holy Week, full of our contributions. The story behind the mite boxes goes back to a parable in the gospels of Mark and Luke of the widow's mite – that the widow's very small contribution was as significant as a large contribution from a wealthy person, because it was a greater proportion of her net worth.

Looking back at it, it appears that my memories of the actual holiday of Easter consist of two very specific, distinct events, which share the elements of love and family.

The first memory has been enhanced by repeated viewings of a movie film my dad shot on Easter morning when I was three years old and Rob was six. There we are in the silent world of 8 mm film, sleepy eyed, in our pajamas, obviously having been aroused from sleep, for the sole purpose of having Dad film our hunt for what the Easter Bunny might have left us. The film shows us peeking in and out of closets, under beds, in the oven, and at various other spots in the apartment. There really could not have been many spots to look, it was only a four room apartment, but to a kid on a treasure hunt it was big.

Finally, the camera catches my face as I slide open a closet door to find the basket. My smile spanned from ear to ear, and my eyes seemed to be twinkling. When my kids first watched that film, they all loved seeing that smile, but then they immediately, in unison, broke into a sympathetic sigh when they caught sight of the basket. It was a very simple wicker basket, with a handful of plastic grass, a small chocolate Easter bunny, and two cupcake holders with jelly beans.

Their minds contrasted my treasure to the baskets that they had received as kids, complete with toys, CDs, and enough candy in each of their baskets to serve as dessert at a dinner party. They all felt bad for me, the little kid on the screen, who was holding this Charlie Brown Christmas Tree version of an Easter basket. Yet, I felt no such emotional pain. I was as happy looking at the film as my smile on the screen indicated I was on that Easter morning. For the next few frames of the film showed my brother, just as happy with just as humble a basket, and then the face of my parents, who were beaming at how happy they had made us with our simple prize.

The next part of the film pictured the whole family, dressed in our Sunday best, with Mom wearing a beautiful Easter hat, and Dad, Rob and I both in suits, getting ready to go to Mass. The film picks up later in the afternoon, showing a gorgeous fresh ham coming out of the oven and being placed on a table, with all the other components of what constituted an Easter feast.

That film, and the experience of watching it with the next generation, highlighted for me why my childhood in Brooklyn was so special. It was never about how big the basket was, or how much candy we got. It was always about the love and the family. We were innocent, and we bought the story about the Easter Bunny. We didn't have much, but we had nothing to compare it to, so we didn't know that we didn't have much. We were taught, through custom, to go looking for a prize left to us by a special character, and we did. And when we found it, we were ecstatic, and exhibited our joy by smiling, laughing, and hugging our parents, which was probably part of the plan all along.

My second memory of Easter, which is a very distinct set of circumstances, shares the elements of love, family, and appreciation for what we had. One of my dad's sisters, Aunt Carmela, had moved to Virginia to raise her family, her husband having come from the Chesapeake Bay – Virginia Beach area. I'm sure it only happened for six or seven years, but looking back at it, it seemed like an annual event throughout my childhood, that we went to Virginia for Easter, to share it with Aunt Carmela, Uncle Al and their children, Mary Jane, Kathleen, Camille, and James.

The trip to Virginia was as big an event as the stay there. My memories are that my aunt could not purchase any "real Italian" products down in Virginia, certainly not like what was available in New York. So my parents packed the car with tomatoes, sausage, pepperoni, cheeses, cakes, cookies, and every other Italian delicacy you could think of. And it wasn't just my parents. I remember that Uncle Frank and Aunt Nellie also made the trip, as did Aunt Josie and Uncle Jerry, and Aunt Ang. And everybody who went brought a little bit of Brooklyn and the family with them.

The prize item which made the trip was the Easter Meat Pie (Pizza Rustica). It is a traditional Easter dish that should probably be banned by the American Heart Association. As you can see from the recipe which follows this chapter, it includes a dozen eggs (eggs being the central ingredient of almost every Italian Easter delicacy) and generous portions of ricotta, provolone, grating cheese, mozzarella, ham, soppressata, ricotta salata, and salami. The delivery of that Easter Pie to Virginia and its unveiling seemed to be as significant as when Charlton Heston brought down the two tablets with the Ten Commandments from the mountaintop.

The second prize, which Rob and I liked even better than the meat pie as kids, was a rice pie that my mom and her mother made, which was a recipe handed down to them from Grandma Millie's family. The attraction to us, as kids, was that it was a sweet treat and it contained real Anisette. We just couldn't get enough of that baby! I still make the Easter Meat Pie and Rice Pies today and enjoy them with my kids and family. But as I get older, every year, the joy of making it, and thinking about my mom and her family, becomes more and more important than the joy of eating it. I hope you can appreciate what I am saying. I think you can.

Now, besides packing all the Italian foodstuffs, and the clothes we would need for our three or four day stay, we needed to pack food for the trip. This was the late 1950s-early 1960s, and my dad was at the wheel. It was a good nine hour trip, because I-95 didn't exist yet, and there was no stopping at McDonald's, or any other place. Dad was a stern taskmaster in general and road trips were no exception. When Dad got us all in the car and on the road, we only stopped for gas. That meant that Mom packed enough food for the trip (and for anybody else we met along the way who wanted a sandwich or a cup of coffee). There was always a Thermos of coffee, a cake (cut into single portions), and sandwiches, plenty of sandwiches, Eggplant Parmigiana being the favorite.

There was no Chesapeake Bay Bridge Tunnel at the time, which meant that to get to Virginia we needed to take a ferry over Chesapeake Bay. As a kid I was amazed that we were going on a boat which we actually drove our car onto! It was a big deal if we just missed the ferry, because we would have to wait almost an hour for the next one. Once on the boat, it was an educational experience. After Dad parked the car, we got out and walked around the ferry. For Rob and me it was our first exposure to blatant segregation. The restrooms and the water fountains on the ferry were marked: White or Colored. We weren't in New York anymore.

When we got to Virginia the joy of the family reunion was palpable. The calendar said it was Easter, but everybody hugged and kissed like it was New Year's Eve, and then when the Meat Pie and other goods started to get unwrapped it was like Christmas morning! Everybody remarked at how big all the kids got, and shared stories of what happened over the past year, and eventually shared all the stories of what had happened over all the years. Part of the fun was mocking (all in good nature) our Virginia relatives' southern accent, complete with "You all," and their making fun of our New York accent, which sounded completely natural to us.

And it didn't stop when evening came, because no hotels were involved. Oh, no. All the guests from New York were divvied up between Aunt Carmela's house and one of Uncle Al's relatives' houses, and you shared a bed with someone, or got a couch, or the floor with a blanket. And we all loved it. Then, when morning came, it was time for the Southern branch of the family to make breakfast: Buttermilk biscuits, bacon, eggs, and pancakes, and always a good, strong pot of coffee.

No trip to Virginia was complete without doing a little crabbing in pursuit of those famous Chesapeake Blue Claws. They did their crabbing a little differently than we did up North. When we went crabbing in New York, it meant a trip to one of the bridges on Cross Bay Boulevard that crossed Jamaica Bay, either the Concrete Bridge or the Steel Bridge, or the First Bridge or the Second Bridge, depending on who you were talking to. On either bridge, the ritual was the same; Dad would pack the car with the crab nets, bait (killies), a thermos of coffee, and sandwiches. He would drop us off at a spot with the gear and the grub, go park the car and walk back to join us. You would throw the nets off the bridge, which opened the net doors, and periodically pick up the nets. While you waited for crabs to take the bait, you would also cast a line for blowfish. I was really too impatient for fishing, but Rob and Dad loved it. I remember one time Rob's fishing line started bobbing and he began reeling it in, but whatever was on the line was giving him quite a fight. Finally, as the line came out of the water, we realized he had caught an eel, and a big one at that. All the Italian fishermen next to us started shouting, "Capitone! Capitone!" Finally, some excitement. Well, in Virginia, they crabbed by attaching frozen chicken pieces to a drop line and walking into the water about thirty feet or so. When you felt a tug on the line you slowly pulled it up and netted the crabs.

We also did some sightseeing when we were down in Virginia, and sometimes on the way there or back. I remember visiting Washington DC, and the Naval Academy at Annapolis. I have great memories of seeing Colonial Williamsburg before it became the tourist attraction it is today. And I will never forget the beauty of the Azalea Gardens, and the military discipline and presence of the Norfolk Naval Base. But all that was secondary; the main purpose of the trip was spending time and sharing love with family. When I hear now about families going to Disney World, or on a Caribbean Cruise for the Easter holiday, I think back to how special our annual trips to Virginia were. Originally, I didn't intend on including the annual trips to Virginia in this book, because they didn't take place in Brooklyn. But as I thought about it, they really did. They started in Brooklyn, and they helped take a little bit of that Brooklyn love of family down to Virginia. Love, family, and appreciating what we had. The elements of the magic of Brooklyn and my childhood are getting clearer and clearer to me.

One of the by-products of our annual trip to Virginia was that Palm Sunday became the holiday we celebrated with Mom's family because we weren't home for Easter. It's part of this Italian-American thing: although we lived in the same house and saw each other every day, the earth would have opened and we would have all been swallowed alive if a holiday passed without the family recognizing it by getting together and sharing some special feast above and beyond our normal Sunday gathering. After Mom died, I inherited the honor of hosting Palm Sunday dinner, complete with the traditional Fresh Ham, the Easter Meat Pie, and the Rice Pie. The recipes for these treats follow this chapter, and I even included the recipe for Eggplant Parmigiana in case you are in the mood for a ride and want to take along a few sandwiches.

FRESH HAM

Since we were usually in Virginia for Easter, it became a tradition in our house to serve the Fresh Ham on Palm Sunday. The kids, when they heard "ham", would always ask if this was the pink one or the brown one. Of course, it is the "brown," uncured ham. Because we have about 30 people over to the house for Palm Sunday, I buy a whole fresh ham, weighing approximately 21 pounds. I have the butcher remove the bone and tie the ham. The bone can be used for stock in other meals. Cooking a fresh ham of this size will take 5 ½ to 6 hours, and the ham should be room temperature when you place it in the oven. I also like to stuff and season it, which takes at least a half an hour. So be mindful of how early you invite your company for dinner. You may have to get up around 7 or 8 in the morning to have it ready. But you have to get up that early to go to the bakery anyway on a holiday, or else you will be without Italian bread, or you will have to wait on a very long line.

Stuffing:
Grating cheese
Raisins
Pignoli
Fresh Parsley, chopped
Salt
Pepper
Garlic, diced, be generous

All ingredients are to taste and should be mixed in a small bowl. Start by dicing approximately six cloves of garlic for a full ham, and then add the other ingredients to your taste. Using a long, sharp knife, plunge the knife into the ham in several spots throughout the ham, creating long, deep pockets. Move the knife around inside the pocket, so that it creates a pocket large enough to accommodate your index finger in width. Once you make the cut, the handle of a wooden spoon works well to create a pocket for the stuffing. Fill each of the pockets with the stuffing. Reserve enough of the stuffing, or make more, so that you can rub the entire outside of the pork with the parsley, cheese, salt and pepper. Place the ham in a rack in a roasting pan, fat side up, and cook approximately 5 ½ hours at 350 degrees. The pork is done when it has reached an internal temperature of 155 degrees. Although pork should cook to an internal temperature of 165, remember that it will continue to cook after you remove it, and if you leave it in the oven until it reaches 165, it will be dry and shred. After you remove it from the oven, wrap it in aluminum foil, and let it stand at least thirty minutes, while you eat your first course. That will allow the meat to cool sufficiently so that you can slice it. First remove and slice the skin, and before serving it scrape off all of the fat attached to the skin. Serve with brown, mushroom gravy, and applesauce, white potatoes, sweet potatoes, and stuffed mushrooms.

MOMMA ROSA'S EASTER MEAT PIE

I don't know where this recipe originated from, but I do know that I have this recipe in my mother's handwriting, with her name on it. I have seen, and eaten, a version of this delicacy in many homes and Italian "pork stores." It is called Pizza Rustica in Italian. We grew up calling it Meat Pie. Grandpa Mike was a butcher, so getting the ingredients for this recipe was his job. This treat should be made a day or two before you intend to serve it. Most of the work is in cutting all the ingredients for the filling before you actually start. I took over my mom and dad's tradition of celebrating Palm Sunday at my house, and the Easter Meat Pie is the much anticipated and quickly devoured first course every year. I serve it with several other appetizers, which all complement each other: Italian Tomato Salad, cracked green olives, roasted sweet red peppers, anchovies, and Italian Bread, and of course, Italian Red Wine. I like to eat it chilled; although some people prefer to eat it heated, like a quiche. Either way, Bonna Pasqua!

Crust:
3 ¼ cups flour
1/6 cup oil (about 1.5 ounces)
4 eggs
1 tsp baking powder
Water

Mix all ingredients on board, first placing the flour down, then creating a "well" in the middle and adding the ingredients into the well. Then knead until smooth. Roll out to approximately 1/8 inch thickness, and line oblong glass ungreased pan (13 x 9); save some dough for lattice strips across the top.

Filling:
½ lb provolone cheese, diced (use the real thing, not the slicing provolone)
½ lb ricotta salata, diced
½ lb genoa salami, diced
½ lb ham, diced
½ lb soppresata, sweet, diced
½ lb mozzarella, diced
1 lb ricotta
¾ cup grated Parmesan cheese
7 eggs

Mix all ingredients in large bowl, stir with wooden spoon. Place mixture into pan, lattice top, brush strips with egg yolk. Bake at 350 – 375 for 1 ½ hours.

GRANDMA CAVALLO'S RICOTTA RICE EASTER PIE

This recipe comes from Grandma Millie's Mom, who I only knew as Grandma Cavallo (she was my great-grandmother). This is not a recipe you will find in most Italian cookbooks. Most people make special pies and cakes around the holidays, and Easter is known mainly for Pizza Rustica (Easter Meat Pie) and Pastiera Grana (Wheat Pie), but around our house the Ricotta Rice Pie was the treat we all waited for. Like most Italian families, we celebrated Palm Sunday, and that is when we got to get our first taste, every year, of this specialty. As kids, my brother and I favored the Rice Pie over the Wheat Pie, maybe because it was sweeter, maybe because of the candy look of the nonpareils, or maybe because it gave us the chance to feel like we were having anisette. It is important to make this recipe a day or two before you plan to serve it. It should be eaten chilled, and is served best with a cup of espresso, with anisette and lemon rind, of course! Enjoy!

Pastry:
10 egg yolks (save 8 egg whites for filling)
2 ¾ cups flour
1 ¼ tsp. baking powder
1/3 cup sugar
5 tablespoons margarine

Mix all ingredients on board, add more eggs if necessary. (I put an ounce or so of Anisette into the dough mixture, to highlight the Anisette taste of the pie.) Knead into a ball, place in bowl and chill dough for one half hour before using. Roll out to 1/8 inch thickness and line 9 or 10 inch ungreased pie plate. Save half of dough for top.

Filling:
3 lbs. whole milk ricotta cheese
1 ½ cups cooked cool rice (should be boiled ahead of time)
1/3 cup Anisette (my brother always told my mother there was never enough Anisette no matter how much she used, but truthfully   the amount of this ingredient can vary according to taste. I like to use at least ½ cup.)
¼ tsp. cinnamon
1 ¾ cups sugar
8 egg whites, beaten

Place all ingredients, except egg whites, in large bowl and mix with wooden spoon. In separate bowl, beat egg whites until stiff, then fold egg whites into ricotta mixture. Pour filling into pie crust.

Bake approximately one hour, at 350 degrees

Originally Grandma Cavallo, Grandma Millie and Momma Rosa used to make a top crust to this pie, and then ice it with the following icing, and then sprinkle nonpareils on it. Years later, when Mom had trouble with her hands, the top crust gave way to lattice strips of crust placed over the filling.

Icing:
1 egg white
1/8 tsp cream of tartar
1 1/2 cups powdered sugar

With an electric mixer, beat large egg white, 1/8 teaspoon cream of tartar until frothy. Mix in powdered sugar; beat on high speed until icing is stiff.

This recipe should yield two nine inch pies.

EGGPLANT PARMIGIANA

This is one of those old stand-bys for parties and large holiday dinners, which could be every Sunday when we were kids, and was always a staple when Mom made sandwiches for long road trips, or trips to Yankee Stadium. The eggplants that Dad grew in his Victory garden had a definite sweetness to them. Maybe it's because they were fresh, maybe because they were a little smaller than the ones at the A&P, or maybe, just maybe, because they were Dad's, and the sweetness came from the satisfaction of using home-grown produce. Of my three kids, Jimmy is the Eggplant King. Man, does that kid love this dish. There are several variations of Eggplant Parmigiana. I'm sure that each family had its own version when they emigrated to America, and having grown up with it, that is the version they believe to be authentic. Some people put mozzarella cheese between each layer – that's the way the kids like it, very stringy. As I got older, I found that I enjoyed this dish with more grating cheese (between each layer) and less mozzarella (just on top). My friend, June Mascia reverses my order of "breading"; in fact, she doesn't use bread crumbs. June slices the eggplant about a quarter of an inch thick and then slices that slice down the middle, but not all the way. She places a few tablespoons of raw meatball mixture in the "pocket", coats it with flour, dips it in egg and fries it. From there, the recipe is pretty much the same as mine. Like Lasagna, this is a dish that is a little neater to serve and makes a better presentation if it sets before you cut it. If you are lucky enough that there are leftovers, by any chance, they make for great heroes, heated up and placed inside a loaf of Italian bread. (C'mon now, not a whole loaf per person, although you will be tempted.)

2 medium eggplants, skinned and sliced
Egg
Milk
Bread crumbs
Grating cheese
Salt
Pepper
Parsley
Italian seasoning
Oil
1 pound mozzarella, sliced
Grating cheese

Peel and slice the eggplant, either horizontally or vertically, depending on your preference. The thinner you slice the eggplant, the more breading you will use, making the dish a little crisper and seasoned. The thicker the eggplant, the "mushier" it will be – slice it how you will like it to taste.

Place the slices of eggplant in a colander (I still call it a "scolapasti") placed on a dish, sprinkle the eggplant with salt every few slices. When you have finished slicing the eggplant, place a dish over it, and place a heavy can on top of it. After about 30 minutes you will see that a dark liquid has drained from the eggplant. According to my mom, draining that liquid takes any bitterness out of the eggplant.

In a soup dish, whisk three eggs and a ¼ cup of milk. In another dish mix bread crumbs with salt, pepper, grating cheese, Italian seasoning and parsley. Place vegetable oil in a frying pan and begin to heat it.

Take each slice of eggplant and submerge it in the egg/milk mixture, dredge it in the bread crumbs, and then place it in the hot oil. Fry the eggplant until golden brown, turning occasionally. Place the fried eggplant slices on brown paper or paper towels after you remove them from the frying pan, to absorb any excess oil.

After all the eggplant is fried, preheat the oven to 350 degrees. In a large roasting pan, spread about two-thirds of a cup of sauce on the bottom, and then place a layer of eggplant. Alternate layers of eggplant, sauce and grating cheese, until you reach the top of the pan. Instead of placing the sauce on the eggplant, an alternative method is to dip each slice of fried eggplant into the sauce, letting any excess sauce drip off. Place the sliced mozzarella on the very top layer. If desired, you can garnish the mozzarella with crushed dried basil, parsley or Italian seasoning before placing the pan in the oven. Cook approximately 40 minutes.

Remove the pan from the oven and place on a wooden cutting board. Once the Eggplant is set, you can cut it with a pancake flipper or spatula. Serve portions that are approximately three inches by three inches. They will come back for seconds.

CHAPTER 15

CATHOLIC SCHOOL – PART III

FOURTH GRADE – SISTER SAINT AGATHA

The nun who taught the fourth grade while I attended St. Gabriel's School was Sister Saint Agatha. As I've already told you, I spent a very brief time in her classroom while I was still in the second grade, and it wasn't a pleasant experience. As soon as I got my last report card from Miss Lauro, telling me that I had been promoted from third grade, a feeling started to develop in the pit of my stomach, knowing that at the end of the summer, I would be the property of Sister Saint Agatha.

There were other elements adding to my agony of anticipation, in addition to my personal experience with Sister Saint Agatha. Getting to the fourth grade at St. Gabriel's was sort of a benchmark, a rite of passage, as fourth graders we were the oldest kids on the first floor of the school. And Sister Saint Agatha had a reputation beyond my dealings with her. In the pecking order of nuns at the school, there was Sister Margaret Joseph, the principal, who had her own office (which you never wanted to get beckoned to), there was Sister Saint Agatha, the "Alpha Dog" of the convent if you will, and then the rest of the nuns. Sister Saint Agatha was also my first teacher who had previously taught Rob, and that meant she knew my family, which for a kid could be good or bad. Rob was not a troublemaker and my family was active in the Church, so that was good. But Rob was a very good student also, and that set the bar high for me as I followed behind him.

Geography was added to the curriculum at the fourth grade level, and a simulated trip across the country on the Lincoln Highway (US 30) was used to introduce us to the features of the United States. The Lincoln Highway was the first federal highway built which spanned the entire length of the country, starting at Times Square in New York and ending in San Francisco, crossing through fourteen states along the way. President Eisenhower had championed the construction of the Interstate Highway System, which became law in 1956, and construction was underway to modernize the nation's highway system. I don't believe there was ever a topic I loved more than learning about the Lincoln Highway. It may be the reason that I love road trips to this day. Every day we would transform our desks into make-believe cars and head out along our journey west, bound for San Francisco. The only things missing were Mom and Dad and the Eggplant Parmigian sandwiches.

As we travelled the famous route in our imagination, Sister Saint Agatha would point out the flora and fauna of the area we were driving through, and we would spend time learning about the history of the area, the famous sites there, and its significance to our country. We travelled through the Pennsylvania Dutch countryside in Pennsylvania, the cornfields of the heartland and into Wyoming. It was a fantastic trip. Unfortunately, either we drove too slowly or the road was just too long, because when the school year ended we only got as far as Salt Lake City, leaving the Nevada and California portion of the highway to our collective imaginations.

Early in the first term of that school year, in October 1962, it didn't look like we would ever make our "trip" across America. It didn't even look like we would make it through October. President Kennedy and Nikita Khrushchev, Soviet Premier, were locked head-to-head in an arms confrontation which has come to be known as the Cuban Missile Crisis.

I had never witnessed anything like this before. Our parents and elders all had fresh memories in their heads of World War II and the Korean War and fully expected the worst to happen again. I remember that in the basement of the school there was an area marked with a "CD" sign, designating it as a Civil Defense Bomb Shelter, stacked with containers of water. And I remember taking part in air raid drills, where the nuns would have us kneel on the floor at our desks and put our heads under the upper portion of the desk. How primitive our understanding was, but how blindly obedient we were. Luckily, cooler heads prevailed, the crisis was peacefully resolved and nobody had to learn how badly our bodies would have been shattered and lost as the Formica and flake board of our desks would be no match at all for the bombs.

My final memory of the fourth grade was the death and funeral of Pope John XXIII, who was canonized as a saint in 2014. Prior to the pageantry which followed his death, including the selection of a new Pope, I had not given any thought to the mortality of the Pope or how a new Pope was selected. All I knew about the Pope could be summed up in four short facts: 1) a Pope had given my Cavallo grandparents dispensation to marry, and that was cool; 2) the Pope was infallible, which was drummed into us by the nuns and priests, and which I thought was pretty impressive; imagine never being able to be wrong; 3) because of my dad's work with the CYO Baseball Program he had received a Papal Blessing, which contained Pope John XXIII's autographed photo, and which was framed and hung on our apartment wall, making it pretty special since no one else's picture hung on our walls; and 4) this Pope was loved by the Church congregation for the steps he was taking to make the Catholic religion more meaningful to our everyday lives by removing some of the mystery, like dictating that Mass should be said in English, and the other topics being discussed by the Vatican Council, which was convened by Pope John XXIII but which did not end its business before his death.

FIFTH GRADE – SISTER MARY JOSEPHINE

Entering the Fifth Grade at St. Gabriel's School was another rite of passage. It meant you had made it to the second floor of the school. I was literally an upperclassman, no longer sharing hallways and boys' rooms with first and second graders.

Unfortunately, it did not take long for my Fifth Grade memories to become dominated by the assassination of President

John F. Kennedy. I truly do not think that there could have been a bigger or more passionate response on behalf of the nuns, clergy, and parish in general, to someone else's death the way there was to the death of President Kennedy. When Pope John XXIII had died several months earlier and there were TV specials and special Masses and commemorative prayer cards and books. But when President Kennedy was assassinated it was different. Maybe because he was so young, or because so much had been made of his historic election, or maybe it was the criminal nature of his death and the facts that surrounded it, or the myth that surrounded it, that made it such a huge event.

Kennedy was assassinated on Friday, November 22, 1963 at 1:30 pm Eastern Standard Time. That exact moment in time became fixed in my memory because it was the first event I can remember that caused person after person to say, "I remember exactly where I was at the moment I heard it happened." There would be other moments like that in my life, like the day we landed on the moon, that were so important that everyone remembered exactly where they were, but Kennedy's assassination was the first in my memory. Years later, it remained a focal point in another way, a measuring stick of a person's age: were you born before or after Kennedy was assassinated?

That event became even more bizarre and memorable because two days after Lee Harvey Oswald killed Kennedy, while Oswald was being transported out of the jailhouse he was shot to death by Jack Ruby on live television. I was watching that with my dad and brother and everyone was in shock at what we had witnessed. It was one of the very first historic events caught on film – something that seems to happen all the time now.

The future of the power of television was seen again just a few months later. In February 1964, The Beatles came to New York and made their historic debut on The Ed Sullivan Show. At that time the Sullivan show was a staple of family viewing every Sunday night. The format of the show was more than predictable: every week there was a stand-up comedian, a musical act, a circus act (juggler, dog trainer, etc.), and there were acts that became regulars, like the lovable puppet Topo Gigio ("Louie Mouse"), and Senor Wences, the stage name of the ventriloquist Wenceslao Moreno, who used his hand as the face of his puppet with his thumb forming the lower lip of the puppet's mouth. His signature line, "Kiss me goodnight Eddie," may have become the most repeated line from the show.

The Sullivan show was the prototypical "G" rated entertainment for the family long before a rating system was even necessary, because everything on TV was acceptable for the whole family to watch back then. Consider that they didn't even let "married" couples share a double bed – the master bedrooms of Lucy & Desi and Rob & Laura Petri featured twin beds.

Prior to Sullivan featuring The Beatles, the most famous musical act he showcased was Elvis Presley, beginning with his first appearance in 1956. Careful not to offend anyone, the camera only shot Elvis from the waist up, without recording any of his famous, suggestive, hip gyrations. My how we have changed.

The appearance by The Beatles wasn't suggestive or risqué but created a riot nonetheless. Most of the commotion was created by the teenage girls in the audience who began screaming at the mention of The Beatles, with their volume increasing in intensity with the duration of their appearance. The Beatles may have very well gone on to become the phenomenon they did with or without their appearance on the Sullivan show, but back in 1964 it seemed to be the thing that catapulted them into the mainstream consciousness of every kid in America, changing what we listened to forever.

In April 1964 the rest of the world came to New York, at the New York World's Fair, held in Flushing Meadow, Queens. That caused great excitement and provided a fun place to go for two years. The Fair, open from April to October in both 1964 and 1965, adopted "Peace Through Understanding" as its slogan, but that really didn't mean much to 11 and 12 year old kids at the time. We were much more interested in all of the fun pavilions.

I can't remember exactly how many times I visited the World's Fair, but the number of visits is immaterial; it is the numerous memories I hold which are meaningful.

When Dad would announce a trip to the Fair you could actually feel the excitement run through your body, and it was fueled by the anticipation which was actually a big part of it. In today's world, a child who knew he was going to the World's Fair would go on the Internet and see the entire event, experience all of the attractions in 3-D, and will have heard all of the music before ever getting to the site. We were blessed in our deprivation. Roadside and subway billboards and TV ads, without today's graphics and computer enhancements, bolstered by newspaper and television stories, were all we had to stimulate our imagination, giving rise to anticipation and then exhilaration at seeing the real thing in person. Most of my visits to the World's Fair were with Dad and Rob while Mom was at work. The drive from Brooklyn to Queens was a quick one, punctuated by Dad telling us how great the World's Fair would be and working us up by having us look for the Unisphere from the minute we left Essex Street.

Although the whole World's Fair experience was too great to recite and recapture here, there are several moments that stick out in my mind as special as they relate to my experience of growing up in the 50s and 60s:

The Wisconsin Pavilion – Although there were dozens of great pavilions, seemingly one for every country in the world, every state in the Union, and every large corporation, one pavilion that drew Dad's attention every time was the Wisconsin Pavilion. It was highlighted by a refrigerated truck with a glass side which exhibited what was advertised as the World's Biggest Cheese – a 17 ton block of Wisconsin-made Swiss. Part of the pavilion was a restaurant called Tad's Steaks, where you could get a freshly grilled steak, baked potato and garlic bread for $1.79! Dad loved hot dogs but steak wasn't far behind, and Rob and I knew that every visit to the World's Fair included a trip to the Wisconsin Pavilion and Tad's Steaks.

The Pieta – No visit to the World's Fair would be complete for a Catholic school kid without visiting the Vatican Pavilion and the famed Pieta statue created by the legendary Michelangelo. The Pieta is a renowned statue depicting the Virgin Mary holding the limp body of the crucified Christ. It is a touching, poignant depiction and its significance was drilled into us by the nuns as soon as it was learned that the statue was to be shipped to America for display at the World's Fair. It was the centerpiece of the Vatican Pavilion, and you only got to see the statue from a distance. You were sort of whisked by it on a moving ramp, sort of a horizontal escalator. That was the first time I was ever on a moving sidewalk, and I thought that was as cool as the statue was impressive.

Bell Telephone – It wasn't the Bell Telephone Pavilion that provided a special memory for me. It was its Family Phone Booth. The "booth" was a room that featured three or four seats in front of a console the size of the family TV. But the console was a phone that contained a speakerphone, which was cutting edge technology for 1964. I remember Dad herding Rob and me into one of those booths and telling us to remain quiet while he called Mom at work, and once she got on the phone we all yelled "Hi" at the same time. Mom couldn't understand how she heard all of us at once and that was a moment stuck in my memory when the whole family experienced a Jetsons moment, which was a big part of what the World's Fair was supposed to be about: giving us a glance of tomorrow. I also remember that the telephone company was predicting a time in the future when you could call someone on the phone and see them live on a screen. It took some time but they were right. Many people now regularly see relatives from across the country while talking to them, thanks to Skype or FaceTime on the iPhone.

Ford – Instead of having people ride in trams, Ford actually put you behind the wheel of its various models of cars. When Dad allowed Rob or me to sit behind the wheel, it was a special treat.

GM – This pavilion became a "must see" when we learned my cousin Frank was working there as a Pinkerton Guard. As a kid, I was so impressed that somebody I knew was part of the World's Fair.

Pepsi Cola – Even though we were a Coca Cola family, Pepsi made a big hit, especially with my mother, with its pavilion which was designed and built by Disney. It was the debut of "It's A Small World." After the Fair was over, the attraction was moved to Florida and became one of the most well-known and best-loved rides in Disney World. Try and get that tune out of your head after you hear it for ten minutes.

CHAPTER 16

THE WONDERFUL WORLD OF COLOR

I came to learn and understand the game of poker at a pretty early age because whenever the family got together, which didn't take much of an occasion, sooner or later the men would wind up playing poker, usually while the women washed and dried the dishes in the kitchen. It seemed that cards, whether it was Scopa or Brišc, and especially poker, was considered a man's recreation in an Italian family. When I say that I came to learn and understand the game, I don't mean to say that I fully understood all the nuances of opening, raising, passing, or bluffing, but I did come to learn that those words, and several others, constituted the jargon of the game, and that oft times the game was referred to by the stakes that would be played: "five and ten" or "quarter and a half", the first amount being the amount of the ante and the amount of a first bet, and the second amount being the amount of a raised bet.

There were times when women would play cards at family functions, and that was usually around the "big" holidays, like Thanksgiving, Christmas Eve and New Year's Eve, when everyone was in a really good mood. On those occasions the game would usually be *Sette e Mezzo* (Seven and a Half), an Italian version of Twenty-One, with the magic card being the King of Diamonds, a Wild Card, known as *La Matta*. The game is played with forty cards (Ace through 7 and picture cards, with the picture cards being worth half a point.) Those games were played for pennies and you were allowed to laugh and have fun, unlike the poker games which looked like serious business to a kid.

When the men were playing cards, and the game was poker, things tended to be a little more serious. Remember this was the 1950s and 60s, when it was accepted to smoke in the house and liquor was more widely consumed at family functions. A men's poker game lent itself to smoking and drinking and had

a much different tone to it than a game of Seven and a Half. I
can only imagine that the tone was even more intense when the
neighborhood men got together and played poker. My dad was a
"regular" player in the "regular" Friday night poker game, along
with four or five other men who all lived on Essex Street. One
of the other regulars in Dad's Friday night game was a single
fellow by the name of Marvin who lived in one of the six-family
apartment houses in the middle of the block. I remember as a kid
feeling defensive and proud about the building I lived in, a four-
family house, as opposed to the six-family building, which was
an "apartment house." We were all one big family in our house.
They were "tenants."

On October 10, 1964, a Saturday, my dad had to go to Marvin's
apartment to give him something. I vaguely remember, or seem
to think, that it was $20 that my dad borrowed at the game the
night before and was repaying. I get the feeling that money was
involved because when we got to Marvin's apartment the men
shuffled me off to the living room to watch TV while they stayed
in the kitchen and discussed "business." Twenty dollars seemed
like decent money to a kid in 1964, considering that I remember
the rent my parents paid my grandparents was $60 a month, and
that was the rent set by the OPA (Office of Price Administration),
a Federal agency started during World War II to prevent wartime
inflation, and then continued under Rent Control guidelines.

I didn't mind being sent to the living room because the
Yankees were on, playing the Cardinals in Game Three of the
World Series, AND Marvin had a color television, a bit of a luxury
in 1964 which hadn't hit our household yet. Dad kept telling
everybody he was waiting for them to perfect it before he bought
a color television. When I turned on the set, the top of the ninth
inning had just ended. The score was tied, 1-1, and the game was
being played at Yankee Stadium. That was the first time I had
ever seen a baseball game in color. Having been to many games,
I knew what the Stadium looked like live, but having only seen
games on television in black and white, I knew instantly that this

was one of those special moments when God gives you a gift. There I was with the ability to see the blue Yankee pinstripes and the deep red colors of the Cardinals' uniforms, the reddish brown clay and the emerald green of the grass on the field, the mosaic of the outfits in the grandstands, and that special color of green that was Yankee Stadium, the result of the patina on all that copper. Every Sunday night as I watched the fireworks on our little television screen explode in shades of gray over Cinderella's Castle, while the Disney singers sang about the wonderful world of color, I imagined what color television would be like. Now I was finally getting a glimpse.

I remember the announcer saying that the Cardinals were bringing in a knuckleball pitcher, Barney Schultz, to face the Yankees, and that Mickey Mantle was leading off the bottom of the ninth. I remember laughing at the name Barney Schultz, because I already thought the name "Marvin" was funny and odd to me, and there I was in his apartment and now Barney Schultz was going to pitch to my hero in Yankee Stadium, the cathedral of baseball. As an eleven year old, I saw humor in that.

Mantle greeted Schultz' first pitch by sending it into the famed rightfield "porch" at Yankee Stadium and the fans went wild, and so did I. My hero had done it again. Long before Derek Jeter and Scott Brosius would call upon the mystique and aura of Yankee Stadium to hit late inning home runs against the Arizona Diamondbacks in the 2001 World Series, Mickey Mantle was building that mystique and instilling that aura back in 1964. I watched the ball sail into the seats and Mickey break into his famous home run trot with his head down. I knew as he rounded third base, Frank Crosetti would pat him on his behind, but I had never seen it in color. To make the moment even more special, Mantle's home run was the 16th he had hit in World Series games, and that broke Babe Ruth's record of 15. I knew as I ran into the kitchen to share the news our beloved Yanks had won another World Series game that I had just seen something that I would remember for the rest of my life, and I have never forgotten one moment of that afternoon.

Years later, as a result of my involvement in youth sports and charity work with athletes, I met Barney Schultz. My mind immediately leapt to that magical moment in October 1964 and I wanted to tell him about it. But from my experiences watching my baseball player friends like Ryne Duren and Mudcat Grant patiently listen to fans tell them stories they had heard a thousand times, I thought discretion was the better part of valor and spared Mr. Schultz my memories,. However, as we was engaging me in conversation, my mind saw him in a Cardinal uniform delivering that famous knuckleball that Mickey deposited into the famous rightfield short porch in Yankee Stadium and I couldn't help but smile.

CHAPTER 17

MRS. FOX AND CRAZY ELVIS

The only building that stood between our house and the apartment building that Marvin lived in, was owned by the mysterious, nefarious Mrs. Fox. Looking back at it now, I am reasonably sure that Mrs. Fox's building was structurally the same as the house I lived in, but back then the tales told by neighborhood kids, bolstered by the overgrowth of weeds in front of the building and Mrs. Fox' seedy appearance, combined to make her building the haunted mansion of Essex Street. Right there between 712 and 718 Essex Street stood 1313 Mockingbird Lane. No one dared go into Mrs. Fox's alleyway (the Brooklyn term for a driveway that ran along the side of the house to the garage). If a Spaldeen went into anybody else's yard or driveway you went to get it. But a ball that went onto any part of Mrs. Fox' property was deemed gone forever. To my memory, nobody, not even the bigger kids, would go get it.

As I remember it, something had happened to Mr. Fox, accounting for his absence, and that same "something" had affected Mrs. Fox. Whatever it was, you couldn't let her touch you or "something" would happen to you. Nobody ever saw anybody else go in or out of Mrs. Fox' four-family house except Mrs. Fox. And if you saw her, you would immediately turn your eyes away for fear of having her see you. I never really knew who lived in that building with her, or that she was indeed a bad person. But neighborhood lore had the neighborhood kids treating her like the bubonic plague. If she were walking down one side of the street, I would immediately cross the street. A ten-year old kid in that neighborhood who wanted to live to be an eleven-year old kid did not take chances with Mrs. Fox.

Looking back on it now, I imagine that our own imaginations comprised the largest component of the Mrs. Fox Fear Factor. She was different than our Moms and Grandmas. She had the name of an animal. Her house was overgrown with weeds. The fear that she struck in our hearts was the product of the condition of her house and our childhood naiveté. She was the natural person to assume the role of the ogre in our fairy tale existence as kids in Brooklyn. The existence was fairy tale, but the fear was real.

With all that being said, believe it or not, Mrs. Fox was not the most feared person of my childhood. That honor belonged to a street skell that we all called "Crazy Elvis" although I don't think anybody knew the guy's name, not even him. Crazy Elvis was my worst nightmare.

Elvis would roam the streets pushing a shopping cart filled with plastic bags, soda and beer bottles that he was collecting for the deposit, (2 cents for small bottles and 5 cents for large bottles) and other assorted items he had pulled from people's garbage cans, with visions of turning them into treasure. Unlike Mrs. Fox, who at least had a home in our midst, Elvis only existed, to our knowledge, pushing that cart in the street. That was part of the problem. We could avoid Mrs. Fox by staying clear of her house and yard. Crazy Elvis came to you. We couldn't really avoid him because we never knew when he was going to show up. So, he was either right there on the block or in your mind because you knew he could be turning the corner at any minute.

He was totally disheveled, with long, straggly, greasy hair and a beard that matched. His clothes were dirty rags. His shoes were shells of their original condition. His fingers and hands were grimy looking. He looked like he had never bathed in his life. We could only imagine the stench that matched his appearance because none of us ever dared get close enough to experience that. He rambled on and on as he walked the street looking for items to collect. Every so often he would raise his voice, shouting at no one in particular.

I remember that when any of us would spot him turning the corner onto our block, our equivalent of an all-points bulletin would be issued with kids whistling and signaling to each other to vamoose. All of the houses on Essex Street were built similarly to the extent that we all had vestibules – the area between the outside door and the inside door that contained the mailboxes and the bells to the respective apartments. Someone coming to visit you would enter the vestibule and ring your bell. In order to gain entry to the house, the host would have to ring a buzzer allowing the inside door to be opened. It was actually a very civil and safe approach. Guests would not have to wait out in the elements, and yet could not gain entry until the host "accepted" them. Well, those vestibules became our sanctuaries when an Elvis warning went out. They shielded us from Elvis, while allowing us to hide in anonymity and not admit our fear to any elders. We would all scatter to our vestibules, or to the vestibule of the nearest friend or relative. I remember I would slide the door curtain aside a few inches every few seconds to determine Elvis' location. If he was within fifty feet of the building, sensing immediate danger, I would ring the bell for entry beyond the vestibule, or key in.

I don't know what the cause of Elvis' "craziness" was, but he would scream and curse at all the kids on the block. I remember experiencing several people who exhibited some very strange behavior back in the late 1950s, like screaming out loud or talking to themselves. I sort of remember the grownups telling us that those people were "shell-shocked," that they were casualties of the War, and left it at that. I came to learn that shell-shocked was a term coined in World War I, and that World War II soldiers suffering those symptoms were said to have Combat Stress Reaction. We now call that condition Post-Traumatic Stress Syndrome.

I don't think Elvis presented any real danger to any of us. The story that struck fear into all of us, besides his appearance and conduct, was that he supposedly pulled out a long knife one afternoon while chasing kids down the block. Whether that was actually true or not, the existence of the story taken together with his looks and ranting was enough to make all of us scatter as soon as we heard the wheels of his shopping cart turn the corner on Hegeman Avenue or New Lots Avenue.

After I moved away from Brooklyn, and time passed, I thought I had forgotten about Crazy Elvis, and the way he made my heart pound. Then when I was watching *Home Alone*, I had a flashback when I saw Macaulay Caulkin react to his elderly neighbor, Old Mr. Marley, whom his older brother made him afraid of. Maybe there is a Crazy Elvis in the back of every little kid's mind, and maybe it was just a guy who the older kids made us afraid of.

CHAPTER 18

CATHOLIC SCHOOL – PART IV

By the time I had reached Sixth Grade I was able to discern definite differences between what my life as a Catholic school student was like as opposed to those of my friends attending PS 202. It's a pretty well-known statement that elementary school education is all about "the three Rs: reading', 'riting, and 'rithmetic." In Catholic school it is four Rs, with RELIGION being first, foremost, and present throughout the teaching of all the other subjects. I venture to say that when public school kids studied and learned American History they were not taught about Saint Isaac Jogues and his fellow Jesuits who became known as the North American Martyrs.

One of our "text" books was the Baltimore Catechism, and every child in the school was expected to memorize the questions and answers which comprised that book. To this day, I still remember most of them, especially those at the beginning of the book, which were drilled into us. From memory, here are the first four questions and answers:

1. Who made us?

God made us.

2. Who is God?

God is the Supreme Being, infinitely perfect, who made all things and keeps them in existence.

3. Why did God make us?

God created man in his own image, in the image of God he created him, male and female he created them. God made us to show forth His goodness and to share with us His everlasting happiness in heaven.

4. What must we do to gain happiness in heaven?

To gain the happiness of heaven we must know, love, and serve God in this world.

Our teachers were not certified educators but, except for Miss Lauro, were nuns who devoted their lives to Christ and the Church. We were taught religion and we were taught discipline, no doubt about that, and we were provided with a no-nonsense approach to education. We were taught the tenets of Catholicism including the seven sacraments and the sacred mysteries which the religion held dear, including the transubstantiation (the changing of bread and wine into the actual body and blood of Christ). But looking back on it, it seems like every time a nun didn't know the answer to a question, like the square root of three, it was deemed to be a sacred mystery!

SIXTH GRADE – SISTER ANNE CARMEL

As I entered the sixth grade, it was to be a little bit of a different experience for me. Rob had been accepted to Brooklyn Technical High School, following his dream of becoming an engineer, which meant that I would be in school without him for the first time. Also, a new nun was assigned to the sixth grade that year, Sister Anne Carmel, so we were entering school without any scouting report. Was she stern, lenient, young, old? How much could we get away with? How much homework would there be? There was no track record for us to study. As it turns out, Sister Anne Carmel was rather young but rather stern, and my memories of the sixth grade are not dominated by her, but rather by the beginning of the end of my East New York childhood experience.

Johnny Chisefsky, who was my "best friend forever" as a kid, long before BFF or texting were ever dreamt of, moved to Florida with his family, vacating the old apartment at 688 Essex Street where I first lived. To give you an idea of how close Johnny and I were you need to know that we were "blood brothers." We heard it somewhere in the street that if we exchanged our blood we would be tied together for life, so we found a way to scratch each other's forearms deep enough to draw blood and then held the "wounds" against each other so that our blood was "mixed.

That same year, Aunt Antoinette and Uncle Al, who lived downstairs at 688, moved to Virginia, near his family and Aunt Carmela. That left 688 Essex Street vacant, and the family sold it to the church, which knocked down the building and paved over the lot and Dad's original Victory Garden to make the schoolyard that much bigger. I remember the day they demolished the building. Dad was in tears, as were his brothers and sisters, which honestly didn't take much – they cried at any story or event involving the family, and I inherited that emotional trait. Dad was able to salvage the house number "688" and the door sash from the building and held on to that as a priceless relic of the house he and his family grew up in.

Other sixth grade memories include my participation in a citywide spelling bee and making it to the third round before being knocked out by the word "construe" which I had never heard before and had misspelled by guessing "constrew." I never spelled that word wrong again. The fact that I was selected to participate in the spelling bee was a testament to my parents' stress on education, which lit a fire, creating within me an insatiable appetite to read and learn. I know I have stated several times how my dad made everything into a learning opportunity. But it was more than that. Both he and my mom always emphasized the importance of learning – and not just what you were being taught in school. Learn every day. Observe. Ask questions. Read. Read. Read.

On that note, they made appropriate reading material available to me at all times. They subscribed to *Highlights*, and then *The Best in Children's Books*, and supplemented that with classics and an encyclopedia. *Highlights* was a treat to receive every month, with features like Goofus & Gallant (teaching you right from wrong), The Timbertoes, and The Bear Family, and we all loved to try and solve the Hidden Picture Puzzle. *The Best in Children's Books* was a great series of hardcover books that featured both classic and new children's stories, including fairy tales and features. The books were filled with illustrations by artists who became quite well known, including Andy Warhol.

From the time I was old enough to remember, my bedroom always contained a bookshelf. I remember my mom teaching me to treat books with respect, and telling me that "a book is your best friend." I became a reading machine. I read every billboard we passed while driving, every ad in the subway, and labels on cans. I read every book I could get my hands on. I remember, no joke, when Mom said it was time for lights out and closed our bedroom door, I would get out of bed, take a book, lie on the floor and try to read by the light coming through the crack under the door!

SEVENTH GRADE – SISTER MARY JUDITH

The beginning of seventh grade was occupied with the buzz that Pope Paul VI was coming to America, to New York to be exact. It would be the first time a Pope had ever come to America. He was to arrive at Kennedy Airport during the first week of October 1965, and that did not give us much time to prepare his welcome. On the morning of his arrival, the entire pupil population of our school, as well as that of all the other Catholic schools in New York City, was herded onto school buses and we were brought to various spots along the Pope's route from Kennedy Airport to New York City. I remember being brought to an area along the Belt Parkway just west of Cross Bay Boulevard, where we would stand on the side of the road to await the motorcade taking the Pope from Kennedy to the United Nations. After standing on the side of the road, with thousands of other students all decked out in our Catholic school uniform best, we saw several New York City Police Department motorcycles pass, and then two black Cadillac limousines, followed by several more police motorcycles. We all raised our arms and our voices, cheering the Pope's arrival and quick passing. That was it. We had "seen" the Pope and witnessed a part of history. Back on the bus and back to school.

While I was in the seventh grade, which covered the time from September 1965 to June 1966, elements that comprised my special little world continued to break down. Johnny Chisefsky and Aunt

Antoinette had moved, then Danny Rizzi and his family moved to Florida. Frank the Barber had passed on. Local shops which been there all my life changed hands. Monsignor Cavanaugh, the pastor of St. Gabriel's, died, and we were now led by Father Tully. Then Sister Margaret Joseph, our principal, left, replaced by Sister St. Agnes. In October 1965, my beloved Yankees failed to make it to the World Series for what seemed like the first time in my life. What the heck was happening?

I remember hearing the song *The Eve of Destruction* by Barry McGuire and relating to the lyrics as they detailed my generation's fears and concerns, stimulated by the Vietnam War, the Cold War and the Civil Rights Movement. I had to share it with someone who mattered, and I remember playing the record for my seventh grade nun. It was probably one of the first signs of a growing social conscience, and the loss of another level of innocence, eating away at the magic of childhood. During that year another incident occurred that shook that feeling of safety we had all shared while playing in the streets and schoolyards of our youth. I was in the schoolyard playing a game of touch football ("two hand touch") with my friends and cousins, and we were using the real leather "Duke" football Dad had gotten me. About a half hour into the game, we were approached by several teenagers whom I didn't recognize from the neighborhood. They entered the schoolyard and pulled out a switchblade, demanding the football. I turned and threw the ball into the locked yard of the rectory, and at that moment I heard my Aunt Ang's voice calling me. She happened to be walking down the block. The teenagers ran away, and I ran to the safety of Aunt Ang.

Not everything that happened during my seventh grade year was negative. Every year the New York City Fire Department sponsored an essay contest. Students throughout the city were asked to submit essays on fire safety. Three winning essays were selected from each grade by borough, but no one had ever won from St. Gabriel's. It just became part of our English curriculum to write the essays and submit them. Then in the seventh grade

I received a letter from New York City Mayor John Lindsay advising me that my essay had been selected as a winning entry. I was invited to a medal ceremony at City Hall and I was allowed to bring my parents and one additional guest. I selected Father Farrugia. It was big news at the school. I guess it was the start of my writing "career." I remember attending the ceremony in front of City Hall. During the ceremony the heavens opened up, and we wound up finishing the ceremony inside the City Council chamber. Afterward we all went to Chinatown for an authentic Chinese luncheon.

CHAPTER 19

STREET GAMES

As children in Brooklyn in the late 1950s and early 1960s, we didn't have the multitude of diversions available to today's children. But that didn't mean we didn't have things to do. When you were old enough to play in the streets there were plenty of other kids around and plenty of games to play. In fact, the number of games we played seemed endless, limited only by our collective imaginations. Most of the games revolved around a Spaldeen, that soft, pink, hollow, rubber ball that was a constant companion of every Brooklyn kid in the 50s.

If you could get enough kids together, which never really seemed to be a problem, the king of the street games was stickball. You didn't need much to get this game going. The street provided the field, with a sewer cap, or man-hole cover, as home-plate, and one sewer cap down was second base. For bats, most of us used old broom handles we had swiped from the house, or salvaged from a garbage pile, or maybe even a shovel handle. A little bit of black tape around it, if you were lucky enough, and you had your bat. The pitcher would throw the Spaldeen to the batter on one bounce and the rest pretty much followed the rules of baseball, with adaptations for the urban street scene. Cars parked in the street also served as first and third base, and building walls served as foul lines. If you hit the ball on the roof of a building it was an out, and sometimes it ended the game, unless someone had another Spaldeen, or one of the group was daring enough to go up on a roof. There were other game-enders too, like breaking a window.

But the real game-ender for us, on Essex Street, was hitting Blackie's car. Blackie was a real smooth guy who owned a white Cadillac, the only guy on the block who owned a Cadillac, and a new one every year at that. Everybody else on the block owned Chevys, or Buicks, at best. And Blackie's car had an alarm that went off if you hit the car. The story that circulated amongst us was that Blackie was "connected", and none of us wanted to upset Blackie. If you hit his car, and the alarm went off, the streets were clear of kids faster than if an Air Raid Alarm sounded!

There were other versions of stickball that became popular because you only needed two guys to play. One was Balls and Strikes, which was played in the school yard, using a strike zone chalked onto the side of building, which really got the custodians and the priests ticked off. Another version did away with the need for a pitcher with the batter throwing the ball up in the air and then hitting it, fungo style.

Part of the fun of the games in the street was choosing sides. That was a game in itself. All the kids who wanted to play got together and two "captains" would each pick one kid at a time, with alternating picks, until everybody was picked. Who got to be captains was the real life demonstration of Darwinian selection. All the kids knew who the best players were and usually without much discussion the captains came forward to start the selection process. It was usually at this time that the worst athletes would yell "NO CHUCKING!" which meant that once the teams were selected you couldn't "chuck" a kid off the team so that the good players would get up more frequently. Once that was settled, one of the captains would toss a bat in the air for the other captain to catch. Then the captains would alternate gripping the handle of the bat, either with a full fist or a scissor-grip with two fingers until one of the captains got to the nub of the bat, making him the winner, BUT the other captain got one chance to win by trying to kick the bat out of his hands. I was not old enough or athletic enough to be one of the captains, but I did avoid the ultimate street dis of being picked last.

After the sides were chosen, the captains would make up their line-ups. While that was happening each of us would call out who we were for that game. The most common call you heard was "I'm Mickey Mantle!" Only the worst couple of kids couldn't call that out – there was an unspoken accepted protocol.

Whoever wasn't quick enough to claim to be Mantle had plenty of other heroes to be on a particular day, but Mickey was clearly our favorite.

Other baseball-themed games did away with the bat, and we just used our hands. We played punchball, (making a fist to hit the Spaldeen), or slapball, using an open hand. Both of those were played in the schoolyard, using the lines of the basketball court as the foul lines. Then there was Triangle, which we played in the street, curb to curb, with one curb cut being first base and another acting as third. We also played Off-the-Wall, where the team that was "up" (even if it was only one person), would throw the ball off a building, usually the school, and the fielder, who would have to stand a certain distance back, would try to catch the ball "off the wall." The number of times the ball bounced before the fielder caught it, determined if it was a single, double, triple or home run, but the ball had to past a certain distance on a fly to be a hit.

Then there was my personal favorite, which drove my grandfather Mike crazy: Stoopball. You could play the game by yourself as a challenge to see how many points you could get before being "out," but the game was usually played by two people against each other. The person who was "up" would stand about ten feet away from the stoop, usually behind a recognizable line, like a line in the sidewalk and would throw the Spaldeen against the stoop, and it would fly back at him. If he caught the ball on one bounce it was worth five points, if he caught it on a fly it was worth ten points. But if the ball hit the point of a step, and came back at him like a line drive, it was worth a hundred points if he caught it. If you failed to catch the ball before it bounced a second time, you were out, and the other player was up. You usually played to either 500 or 1000 points.

My grandfather Mike was not a sports guy. The sound of the Spaldeen bouncing up off the front door of the building made him crazy. In fact, just the sight of us playing on his stoop, would have him chasing us, yelling that we were loosening the bricks.

We just ran down the street and picked someone else's stoop, and resumed play as soon as possible.

My dad would always tell me that if I was looking for something to do after school, after I got changed from my school uniform, just put a Spaldeen in my pocket, go down to the schoolyard and start throwing the ball against the wall – within minutes I would have a game going. And he was right. There were the games I already described and much simpler ones, like: handball, Chinese handball, boxball, baseball boxball, and even the simplest: Hit the Penny, where the two players would stand separated by two flags of sidewalk and would place a penny on the "crack" dividing the two flags; the players, using a Spaldeen would take turns trying to hit the penny, with each hit being worth a point and if you got the penny to flip it was worth two points, and besides aim and coordination there was strategy involved: you didn't want to hit the penny too hard because that would drive it closer to your opponent, making it easier for him to hit. Most of our activities were not organized by any leagues, and had no referees other than the participants ourselves. We learned to regulate ourselves and we even learned some new words, like "do-over" and "hindu" which was what a player called out to get a do-over, if a ball took a crazy bounce, or some other weird event happened.

There were other games we played, without the Spaldeen, like two-hand touch football, ring-a-levio and Johnny on the Pony, and then there was Skully. Skully was huge in our neighborhood. It was played in the street, on a "playing board" that we drew with chalk. The size of the "board" and its components varied depending on who drew it, but basically, the board was approximately four feet by four feet and contained thirteen numbered boxes, twelve of which (boxes 1 – 12) were located along the perimeter of the board, with the 13th box being located in the center of the board, surrounded by a "dead man's zone" or "skull." Outside the board, about two feet away from Box 1, was the start line.

Each of the players used a bottlecap, which was given weight by filling it with melted wax. The order of play was determined using a choosing rhyme which was a ritual in itself. All of the players would gather in a circle and put both of their fists into the middle. One of the players would start by reciting a choosing rhyme and tapping each fist in clockwise order, starting with his own, to the beat of the rhyme, and the player whose fist he landed on when the rhyme ended was selected and went first, and so on until the order was complete. There were several choosing rhymes, all handed down by street legend, but these are a few I remember:

Eenie, meenie, minie mo
Catch a spider by the toe
If he hollers let him go
Eenie, meenie, mini mo
My mother said to pick this one
So out goes, Y – O – U!

or
One potato, two potato, three potato, four.
Five potato, six potato, seven potato, more.

or
Ticky, ticky tumba, no sir rumba
Otta-botta-butski
Hip-ro-tenda, hocha!

That's the way I remember my dad teaching that last one to me, but I have come to learn that the real words are: Ticky Ticky Tembo No Sarimbo Hari Kari Bushkie Perry Pem Do Hai Kai Pom Pom Nicky No Meeno Dom Barako. It doesn't surprise me that the way we learned it was different from how it was written. For years Dad would sing the first few lines of *Oklahoma*, as "Oklahoma, where the wind goes biddy, boddy, boo!"

Back to Skully. Once the order was determined, each of the players in Skully placed his bottle cap on the start line and flicked the bottle cap with his finger, aiming for Box 1. If the cap landed in Box 1, he got to go again and shoot for Box 2, and so on. You could keep your turn by landing in the next box, or by "blasting" another player's cap, as far away from the board as possible. If your shot didn't blast anyone or land in a Box, then you had to wait your turn to go again. After going from Box 1 to Box 13, you had to return going from Box 13 to Box 1, then right back to 13, and then around the skull, at which time you became a "killer" and would eliminate the other players by hitting them. The last player left won.

We usually played the game on the condition that the winner got to keep all the bottle caps involved in the game. So, at the beginning of the game you might hear the weaker players yelling "No Keeps!" but that condition was never accepted, and it was a status symbol of the street to be walking with a plastic bag full of bottle caps.

When we got real ambitious we might "organize" a bigger game, like baseball or tackle football, and to play those we would go to the empty lot at the corner of Essex and Hegeman, where the old Italian men used to play bocce, and which has now been built on. If the game involved other kids from school, and not just the kids on the block, we would go to Rich Field, which was nothing more than a bigger empty lot between Elton Street and Cleveland Street, between Hegeman Avenue and Linden Boulevard.

After our creativity and energy ended the street games for the day, or the heat of the summer called for a break, we headed to the corner of Shepherd Avenue and Hegeman Avenue for sodas. At the candy store you could get a Cherry Water, or Cherry Lime Rickey or an Egg Cream, but that was good for when you were younger or with your folks. When the "gang" took a break we opted for Julius', the little grocery store on the other corner, where you reached down into the cooler and identified the soda you wanted by the bottle top sticking out of the ice water. Even then the guys were arguing Coke vs. Pepsi.

CLASSIC EGG CREAM

The egg cream is a legendary New York drink, which contains neither eggs nor cream. It was best consumed at a candy store or luncheonette that served fountain soda. This is not one of those recipes that you get creative with. The ingredients are simple, but specific, and the order of "assembly" is important to create the right foam and the appearance of this classic treat. The seltzer that was used back in Brooklyn was fountain seltzer, under pressure, which created the foam. The seltzer by itself was called "Two Cents Plain" which is what it cost for a glass. We used to get seltzer delivered at home in blue siphon bottles, the kind that The Three Stooges used in their food fights. The syrup used was always Brooklyn's own U-Bet.

Tall glass, 12 to 1 ounces
Long spoon
½ cup cold whole milk
Seltzer
2 to 3 tablespoons chocolate syrup

Place the spoon in the glass. Add the cold milk.

Put the seltzer in the glass, under pressure, creating the foam. Add enough seltzer to bring the mixture to about an inch or so from the rim of the glass.

Pour the chocolate syrup into the glass right down the middle of the drink, until the top of the drink hits the rim of the glass. Stir the drink with spoon, keeping the spoon at the bottom of the glass. Remove the spoon and enjoy. This drink is made to be consumed within minutes or it will go flat and lose its appeal.

CHAPTER 20

FOOD WARS

Coke vs. Pepsi. That was the subject of many an argument on the way back to another game as we chugged down our respective favorite. There were very few undecideds. We were a Coca-Cola house. Don't ask me why. I just knew that nothing beat the taste of Coke, especially from those little eight ounce bottles that came out of the vending machines, like the one in the school auditorium, or, more interestingly, like the one in Uncle Al's gas station, which was right next to the calendar with the naked pin-up girls, who appeared to be clothed until you learned the trick of lifting the plastic sheet which was providing an opaque bathing suit.

I remember one year, I think it was 1965, there was a special reason to drink as much Coca-Cola as possible. They ran a promotion with the New York football Giants (although the New York baseball Giants had left for California and were now the San Francisco Giants, everybody felt the need to say "New York football Giants" and people still use that term). Coke placed a player's name, face, and position inside of the bottle cap. We already loved bottle caps to use in our Skelly games, but this gave us a new reason to collect (and a challenge to not bend the cap too much when taking it off the bottle). It was my first effort at collecting sports memorabilia, and playing with it. I wanted to collect the whole set and arrange them on the linoleum floor in football formations. The names of the Giants at that time have stayed in my memory: Y.A. Tittle, Jim Katcavage, Rosey Brown, Joe Morrison.

Coke vs. Pepsi was only one of the food wars we waged. Similar discussions and entrenched positions were held concerning things like soft ice cream (Freezer Fresh vs. Mister Softee), hard ice cream (Bungalow Bar vs. Good Humor), baked goods (Dugan Bros. vs. Ebinger's), and chocolate syrup (Bosco vs. Hershey's vs. Brooklyn's own U-Bet).

And it wasn't just brand names that divided people. Everybody had an opinion on where to get the best pizza (home), the best pastry, the best Italian ices, the best cappauzelle, the best knishes, the best hot dogs, etc. While I'm talking about those types of foods let me share some memories.

Pizza was not the take-out favorite then that it is now. The pizzeria business expanded exponentially after World War II with many veterans returning from Europe with a desire for the tasty treat. Pizza was a dish best made at home. Nobody beat Aunt Josie's or Aunt Nellie's "abeetz." Mrs. Rizzi, whose family was Barese, (and who made the greatest barbequed lamb) made a thick pizza, more like the focaccia which is very popular now, and it was unbelievable. It was at least two inches thick and the bottom crust was crunchy because of the amount of olive oil she put in the bottom of the pan.

There were several pizzerias around then, and everybody had his or her favorite. It was a quick, easy snack after school, at 15¢ a slice and 10¢ for a small fountain soda. It was not unusual for a whole pie to be $1, a lot less than one slice costs now. And the choices were pretty simple: Sicilian or Neapolitan, which many places called "plain" or "regular." If you were ordering a pie to go it would be cheese or anchovy, and the anchovy was just tomato sauce and anchovy. Now your choices are endless, including Hawaiian Pizza with ham and pineapple. Mrs. Rizzi must be spinning in her grave.

Italian ices are another item that has seen remarkable change and growth since I was a kid. In our neighborhood we didn't have stores dedicated to just Italian ices. You went to the nearest Italian bakery for the best ices, and then your choices were pretty much limited to lemon, cherry, and chocolate. Eventually pizzerias started to sell ices and the number of flavors expanded. I remember many a hot summer night when Dad would ask everybody what flavor they wanted. Then he would drive to the Italian bakery on Sutter Avenue and return with the frozen treats for everybody who was sitting outside on the stoop or in their lawn chairs to escape the heat of their apartments. If it was actually Italian pastry that we were after it had to be Ariola Bakery on Rockaway Avenue.

As for hot dogs, the local favorite was Murray's Hebrew National Deli on the corner of Shepherd Avenue and New Lots Avenue, which is also where you went for a "real" Jewish knish. But every so often the urge for Nathan's was too strong to resist. Another favorite was Coney Island Joe's on Linden Boulevard and Stone Avenue where the adults could get a Double Dog.

Eating out at restaurants was a rarity during my childhood. All of my relatives were very talented in the kitchen, and money was too sparse to pay others to make what we made better. I remember that a few times a year when we did go out to dinner, if it was for Italian food, we would go to Carlucci's at 1845 Eastern Parkway (which is now Xin Long Restaurant). Of course, if Dad was in the mood for seafood that he wasn't cooking, it had to be Lundy's Seafood Restaurant or Randazzo's at Sheepshead Bay, or baked clams at Pizza City on Cross Bay Boulevard.

If we went out for Chinese our choices were pretty much limited to the House of Wong, on Cross Bay Boulevard, and the House of Yu, on Linden Boulevard. Whenever somebody mentioned House of Yu to Dad his standard remark was "I'mma fine, how'sa you?" And talking about limited choices, Chinese restaurants in the '50s and early '60s were strictly Cantonese: Egg Rolls, Wonton or Egg Drop Soup, Chow Mein, Chop Suey, Egg Foo Yong, and the like. Szechuan and Hunan had not yet been introduced. Forget about sushi or any Japanese food. It was too soon after World War II. Egg Foo Yong was Rob's favorite and I was stuck on Chicken Chow Mein.If it was bagels and bialys that we were after, there was a little store on the southeast corner of Linden Boulevard and New Jersey Avenue, right next to Food Fair that made the best bialys, and onion wheels!

CHAPTER 21

SIGHTS, SOUNDS, SMELLS AND TASTES

There are certain sights, sounds, smells and tastes that can bring me back to my childhood Brooklyn of the 1950s and '60s in an instant:

SIGHTS:
> DAD'S BLACK & WHITE BUICK CENTURY
> THE DRY ICE IN THE BUNGALOW BAR TRUCK
> A YELLOW FORMICA KITCHEN TABLE
> A CLOTHESLINE FROM WINDOW TO TELEPHONE POLE
> A BOTTLECAP FILLED WITH WAX TO PLAY SKULLY
> THE SYCAMORE TREE SEED PODS, WHICH WE CALLED
> ITCHY BALLS

SOUNDS:
> THE BELLS OF A GOOD HUMOR TRUCK
> TOMATOS HITTING SIZZLING OIL
> THE ROAR OF AN ELEVATED TRAIN PASSING OVERHEAD
> BROOKLYNESE WORDS: BUTTINSKI (a guy who couldn't mind his own business); SKINNY BALINK (person whose friends or family thought he was too thin); JOHNNY PUMP (fire hydrant);
> SALOOGI (a game of keep away)

SMELLS:
> THE LEATHER OF A NEW SCHOOLBAG
> GARLIC FRYING IN OIL
> A NEW SPALDEEN
> BUBBLE GUM IN A PACK OF BASEBALL CARDS
> A CARNATION (like we wore in our lapel for our First Communion)

TASTES:

A GOOD HUMOR TOASTED ALMOND POP
A FIG STRAIGHT OFF THE TREE
POTATO KNISH FROM MURRAY'S DELI
A COMMUNION HOST
LEMON ITALIAN ICES
COCA-COLA FROM A LITTLE GLASS BOTTLE

CHAPTER 22

TELEVISION

I believe television was an invention that impacted the Baby Boomers more than any other generation. It was to us as computers would be to children of the 1980s and 1990s. It was a novelty for our grandparents, a wonderment how a "box" in the living room could bring pictures of people from around the world. To our parents it was a little more widely accepted, but still in its infancy, not to the stage where it could be fully enjoyed, like we Boomers came to know it. At least we thought we had come to fully enjoy it, but amazingly it is still being improved upon, with flat screen TVs, high definition, and now 3-D.

The technology, as new and amazing as it was to all who saw it, was still crude and limited. My recollection is that we had one television set in our apartment, a Stromberg Carlson which occupied a good portion of the living room. The screen was fairly small, like 9 or 10 inches, but it was enclosed in a coffin size piece of furniture – the "console" – that was beautiful by 1950s standards – mahogany or cherry, with doors to keep the screen out of view when not being used.

The actual picture tube was a monstrosity and the set's inner workings: comprised of a number of odd shaped tubes. When the set went on the fritz, Dad would take off the back of the set to reveal all of the different tubes. It was an adventure for us as kids. Looking into the back of the TV was like peeking behind the curtain at the Wizard of Oz. Dad would try to figure, from appearances, which of the bulbs was "dead." He would remove the suspected culprits and we would go to Scharf's Drug Store on Hegeman Avenue where they had a tube tester. To this day I can't figure out the connection as to why the tube tester was in the drug store, but it was. The top of the tube tester had sockets in the various configurations to match the prongs on the bottoms of the different tubes. Dad would place the bulb in the appropriate socket to determine whether it was "dead" or not. If it was, he would open the cabinet below and purchase a new bulb.

The complexity of the inner workings of the TV was matched by the frustration of hooking up the antenna and securing reception. Cable TV and satellite TV didn't exist. Our reception relied on an antenna that was placed on the roof, as was the reception of every other television, making the antenna a mainstay of every roof. Going up on the roof was always Dad's job. Our job was to watch the TV and to yell up to him when the reception was at its best. It became a screaming dialogue of "How's that?" from Dad, followed by "No good" from us, as he continued to move the antenna until the reception was clear, with all "snow" removed, meaning the antenna was aligned in the best spot.

Once the TV was working and receiving clear reception, what it had to offer was another story – a quite limited one, especially by today's standards. Our choices in New York were Channels 2, 4, 5, 7, 9, 11, and 13. They were called VHF channels – standing for very high frequency. The TVs had a separate knob for UHF – ultra high frequency – but there was never any reception. Channel 13 was educational television, which we only watched when our parents made us watch. And I remember watching several pretty interesting educational and informative shows on that channel with Dad. *MisterRogers* was on that channel every morning, but we were not a *MisterRogers* watching family. The broadcast day didn't begin until 5:00 am with a show called *Sunrise Semester* on Channel 2 (CBS) and was off the air after the Late, Late Show. If you had insomnia there were no infomercials, 24 hour news channels, or old movies to keep you company between 1:00 am and 5:00 am, just the test patterns that each channel ran. The broadcast day would start and end every day with the playing of The Star Spangled Banner.

Since there was only one television in the apartment, the family watched together, which meant that all of the shows were family fare. The week's schedule was pretty much a set routine, i.e., *Bonanza, Disney, Ed Sullivan,* and *Dennis the Menace* on Sunday nights. During the afternoons, after school, when we were not out playing, WPIX-TV (Channel 11) ran *The Three Stooges* for a half hour with Officer Joe Bolton and *Popeye* for another half hour with Captain Jack McCarthy. *Abbott and Costello* had a half hour show every afternoon, with Hillary (the beautiful blonde), Mike the Cop, and Mr. Fields (the landlord), and on Sunday mornings there would be *Wonderama, Let's Have Fun* and an Abbott and Costello movie. If you were home from school for a sick day or a holiday, you got to watch re-runs of *I Love Lucy, Amos and Andy, My Little Margie* and *December Bride.* The prime time for kids though was Saturday mornings, when cartoons and kids' shows ruled the air waves. This was before *Dora the Explorer* and even *Sesame Street.* The technology of graphics and animation were not as advanced as they are now, but the list of shows we watched could fill a treasure chest: *The Roy Rogers Show, Howdy Doody, Ding Dong School, Beany and Cecil, Andy's Gang, Cisco Kid, The Flintstones, Jinx the Cat with Pixie and Dixie, Huckleberry Hound, Mighty Mouse, Heckel and Jeckel, Woody Woodpecker, Felix the Cat, Casper the Friendly Ghost, Yogi Bear, Quick Draw McGraw, Dick Tracy, Peabody & Spencer, Snagglepuss, Rocky & Bullwinkle, Courageous Cat and Minute Mouse, Speedy Gonzalez* and *Underdog,* not to mention *Bugs Bunny, Porky Pig, Daffy Duck,* and *Sylvester.*

The TV definitely became part of the culture of the American household during my childhood years. The entertainers that my parents and their generation waited on lines for hours to see at the Paramount theatre, like Frank Sinatra, now performed in our living room. Madison Avenue quickly discovered the power of television advertising.

Winky Dink and You was one of the cartoons that aired in the mid-1950s, for five years, and then for several years later on reruns. The premises of the cartoon was that at some point during each episode, Winky Dink needed the viewer to save him by drawing some type of structure, like a bridge, so that Winky Dink could get from Point A to Point B. They built on that premise by selling a plastic shield and set of crayons, instructing the child watching the cartoon to place the plastic over the screen and use the crayons to draw the bridge. My parents never let us buy the plastic. Instead, Dad, an X-Ray technician, would bring home exposed X-Ray films, and Rob and I would draw Winky Dink's survival bridge over some Health Department patient's rib cage.

The plastic and crayons sold to Winky Dink viewers were just the tip of the iceberg for marketing generated by the presence of televisions in homes. Saturday cartoons became vehicles for the sales of toys. Old movies reappeared as new television shows. Then television shows spawned movie versions of the show – like *McHales's Navy*. (The stars would actually show up at the local theaters when the movie hit our neighborhood. I remember, in 1964, Aunt Ang bringing me to the Kinema on Pitkin Avenue to see Tim Conway and Joe Flynn on stage before the movie.) Advertisers enjoyed the new medium, and products were created around the viewing that families were doing.

One of the "new" products was the TV Dinner: fully-cooked, three course meals that included an entrée, a side dish and a dessert, that only required "heating" in the oven. Of course, those dinners were the precursors of all the prepared food being sold today, which is much more conveniently heated for serving because of the invention of the microwave. The first TV Dinner I saw was in my friend Johnny Chisefsky's house. I was over at his family's apartment when it was getting close to dinner time and his mom took TV Dinners out of the freezer. I thought they were the coolest thing, and when I got home I started bugging my dad to get me TV Dinners. He wanted no part of them. But I was relentless in wanting to be cool like the other kids in the block. So, in typical Dad fashion, he bought a TV Dinner for me and one night he told me I was going to have a TV Dinner that night. My excitement was erased when I saw my TV Dinner and then saw the rest of the family being served my favorite dish – Mom's Lasagna. Of course, I wanted Lasagna, but Dad told me that since I wanted the TV Dinner that was what I was eating that night. Salisbury Steak, mashed potatoes and a tablespoon of Apple Crisp was no match for Mom's Lasagna. I don't remember asking for TV Dinners again.

CHAPTER 23

FACTS OF LIFE

WHERE BABIES CAME FROM

Most of the entertainment we enjoyed as kids growing up in East New York was self-generated within our group of friends, at no cost. Every so often though, we would splurge and go to the movies. Once my children got too old to drag them to the Saturday matinees of children's movies, most of which were re-cycled Disney classics from our childhood, I can't remember any of my children asking to go to the movies with their friends on a Saturday afternoon. By contrast, we would get a group of guys together and venture the walk down New Lots Avenue, past the Dutch Reformed Church (and the hundred year old graves), past the Brooklyn Public Library, to the Biltmore Theatre.

For a mere quarter we were treated to a newsreel, one or more cartoons, and the main feature, and sometimes a double feature. Each of my senses still retains memories of the Biltmore. My eyes can still paint a picture of the woman who sold the tickets from that small booth, the tuxedoed ticket taker, the velvet ropes used to control the line, the ornate wall decorations, and the light coming from the matron's flashlight as she patrolled the aisles to keep everyone on his or her best behavior. My nose can recreate the aroma of buttered popcorn, and the scent that is uniquely that of a cinema. My fingers can tell me they remember the crushed velvet maroon seats, the butter of that popcorn, and the experience of digging that last Jujube or Milk Dud out of the box in the dark of the theatre, and then trying to pick it out of your teeth a little later. My taste buds obviously equate the theatre experience with a bucket of buttered popcorn, candy, and a Coke. My ears remind me of the awesome sound of the theatre compared to our little Stromberg Carlsen television at home, with a nine inch screen and a huge console. I can still hear the advertisements promoting the goodies on sale in the lobby, and the coming attractions which always made you want to see the next movie even more than the one you came to see.

One of my earliest memories of attending a movie was on Good Friday in 1961 when my brother took me along with him and his friends to see *Gorgo*, a monster movie. I don't remember the movie too well, but I do remember the lashing we got from Dad that night for going to see an action movie on such a holy day.

I have another memory that was created at the Biltmore, but it had nothing to do with the movie itself. On a Saturday in October 1965, about six or seven of us, at the ripe age of 12, went to the Biltmore to see Steve McQueen in *The Cincinnati Kid*, starring Edward G. Robinson. What makes that Saturday stick out in my mind is the conversation that took place among my friends and me as we waited for the house lights to dim and the coming attractions to start. One of my friends decided that this would be a good time to share with us his understanding of the birds and the bees. He pronounced to the group, all good Catholic boys being educated by the Sisters of St. Joseph, at St. Gabriel's School, the exact location where babies exited their mothers and entered the world. Well, much to our surprise, a few years later we would all come to learn that our friend was correct, or at least I hope all my friends did! But back on that Saturday in the Biltmore Theatre we all told him he was strange, demented and out of his mind, and beat him up for it. It was totally impossible and unthinkable for a baby to come from where he said it did. First of all, there is no way the baby could fit through there, even though none of us had any idea how big "there" was. Second of all, we thought we knew what came out of "there" and it wasn't babies. And third of all, we all knew our parents were lying to us about the stork, because we knew that babies came from mommy's belly. That was what we figured out by ourselves when we were a little older, and it sat much better with us than what our friend was telling us. And to think our parents were probably wondering if we were old enough to see *The Cincinnati Kid*, not knowing we were busily discussing babies and where they came from. And what we were hearing was a lot stranger than Cincinnati!

WHERE BABES WERE

Since Mom and Dad worked every day, and Rob was attending Brooklyn Tech HS, which meant he took the subway, I was a latchkey kid, and was pretty much on my own for a few hours every day after school, as long as I reported to my grandmother when I got home, and let her know where I would be. Funny thing is that "out playing" sufficed as one of the "places." The usual routine was: key in to the apartment, run out of my school uniform, put on jeans, a t-shirt and sneakers, put a Spaldeen in my back pocket, and fly out the door to be with my friends.

But one day when I was in the seventh grade, curiosity (which I had been told many times had killed the cat) got the best of me, and I started to poke around in the apartment in places where I had never been and probably didn't belong. Most of what I found was boring, mundane, everyday sort of stuff. Until I hit the end table on my father's side of the bed in my parents' bedroom. Then and there, additional layers protecting my innocence and naiveté were shed, and my adolescent hormones started to slam dance as I discovered my first *Playboy* magazine.

There in her splendid glory, in a feature on the Bond Girls, was Ursula Andress. After I picked my eyeballs off the floor, I put the magazine back exactly where I found it and raced out to see my friends and share my discovery. I remember going back to that end table for several days in a row after school, repeatedly pleased and amazed that the magazine was still there and that Ursula was still naked. Then one day I got the courage to show the magazine to my friends. We were all giddy and swore each other to secrecy. After that, for weeks, our favorite topic other than baseball was *Playboy* magazine and the actress we called, (with no claim of originality), Ursula Undress.

CHAPTER 24

BUILDING A NEST EGG ONE DOLLAR AT A TIME (IF YOU WERE LUCKY)

New York City has long been recognized as one of the biggest cities in the world, whether its size is being measured from a financial, entertainment, sports, theatre or news point of view, or based on sheer area. Despite the size of the metropolis, it seemed to me back in the 1950s that each few blocks of the city was an entity unto itself. As I said earlier, both my maternal and paternal grandparents lived on the same block as my immediate family, and several aunts and uncles also lived on that block or within one block east or west. Then there was the extended family, or as might be described in today's lingo, the virtual family. (Every time I hear the adjective "virtual" I think of the first times I heard it, from sportscasters proclaiming that two teams were in a virtual tie for first place. I didn't fully understand then what a virtual tie was. To me, either you were tied or you weren't, and for the life of me, I couldn't figure what virtue had to do with any of it.)

One of the attributes of our neighborhood was the working class nature of the people who lived there. Most of the houses were two family homes, semi-attached, sharing a common driveway with the building you were not attached to. Even the four-family homes and the six-family buildings were semi-attached, and down at the end of our street was a ten-family apartment building. Nobody owned any appreciable amount of land to speak of, at least nobody we knew. The fact that the semi-attached four-family houses owned by my grandparents and uncle each had a vacant lot on the side of the building was unusual. The lot to the side of our building contained the garden that was my dad's pride and joy. Having only been born in 1953, I couldn't fully comprehend how close we were as a nation to the end of World War II, so I also couldn't entirely grasp why my father, a World War II veteran of the campaigns in Iwo Jima and Okinawa, took such pride in his Victory Garden. I had no real appreciation yet for the sacrifices made by my parents' generation, or how threatened our way of life was. To me, it was a bunch of tomato plants and squash vines, prettied up by some beautiful but non-fragrant gladiola and poppies, and some very fragrant, but very thorny, rose bushes.

My dad worked for the New York City Health Department, as an X-Ray technician, and then as a Supervisor of Registered Technicians. I remember everybody saying he had a Civil Service job and that he had "benefits", but I didn't have a real appreciation of that as a child. My mom also worked, as a Legal Secretary. She stopped working for a while, I was told, when my brother and I came along, but then went back to work when I went to school. There were many times I resented my mom not being there for me when I came home from school – to listen to a story that would only be important to a little kid and his mom; to instantly share a good report card, or to wipe away a tear caused by some feeling of not belonging or not achieving. Anytime I brought this up, I was reminded how lucky I was to have my grandparents around, and how Mom working allowed me certain luxuries like vacation and "nice" clothes.

My mom and dad were pretty conservative people. Neither of them smoked, and alcoholism was never a fear or a concern in our household, luckily. Grandpa made wine, and then so did Dad, and Dad and his family could certainly consume their share of beer, including half kegs for house parties, but it seemed that everybody knew his or her limit. My brother and I were always dressed nicely, but not overdone, and we did own a car, and we even had an air conditioner in our apartment. It was in my parents' bedroom, and on particularly oppressive nights, my brother and I were allowed to drag a mattress into the room and plop it on the floor, and the four of us slept in cool, harmonious comfort.

My parents also instilled in my brother and me a sense of building a little nest egg, saving for a rainy day. I remember one clear indication of that. Every Thursday a representative of The East New York Savings Bank would visit our school. He would be carrying a small trunk with two big leather straps around it. He would go from class to class and would pass out empty Manila envelopes that were marked "East New York School Savings Program" and contained lines for us to enter our name, address, the name of our school and our grade, and on the bottom portion of the envelope were two squares, labeled "Dollars" and "Cents." When the bank representative came to a room he would hand out the empty envelopes and would collect from the students the envelopes he had distributed the week before, which were now completed and contained deposits into the students' respective accounts. I remember thinking about what stopped this guy from taking that little suitcase full of money one Thursday and not taking it to the bank and not coming back to the school next Thursday.

At one point during the year, the bank sent a photographer to the school. He took a class picture of all the classes that participated in the program, and there would be a banner that said "Honor Thrift Class." At the end of the year, the representative came to our classroom and distributed copies of the photo in a cardboard folder that stated it was printed courtesy of The East New York Savings Bank. He also gave us our "passbooks" so if we wanted to make deposits during the summer we could. Nobody ever talked about withdrawals, only deposits. I remember that Mom and Dad would always send me to school on Thursday mornings with at least one dollar in that envelope. I noticed that other students only put in twenty-five cents or fifty cents, and it made me feel proud of my parents.

I remember going to the bank with my dad one day. That was back in the day when banks didn't have the technology available to us today. There were no ATMs, no drive through tellers and no on-line bank transactions back then. But banks were BANKS. There were no banks that looked like they were converted convenience stores. Banks conveyed a sense of majesty and security. They were all very big on concrete, very big on marble, very big on very high ceilings, very big period. I remember feeling very small in that bank, and I remember looking at the large pillars and the very high ceiling, and I remember looking around for that man with the suitcase, but never finding him.

CHAPTER 25

COMMUNITY COMMERCE

I imagine I'm not alone these days in doing much of my shopping on-line. There is a definite ease involved in researching what I want to buy, comparing prices, ordering, and waiting for the product to be delivered, all without the hassles of traffic, parking lots, going store-to-store, the pressure of salesmen, and the "joy" of schlepping home packages. But it is all so impersonal compared to how business was conducted in Brooklyn during my childhood.

Back then our doorbells would ring on a steady basis, and you were likely to be greeted by any number of salespeople who made their living bringing their products directly to you. Most famous among them were The Fuller Brush Man, The Avon Lady, and the Biangaleen Man.

The scope of The Fuller Brush Man went well beyond Brooklyn. In fact, in 1948 they made a movie called *The Fuller Brush Man*, starring Red Skelton. A female version starring Lucille Ball was released in 1950, called *The Fuller Brush Girl*. The sales force of Fuller Brush Men was descendant from Albert Fuller, a Canadian native, who first developed his line of brushes in 1906. The sales demonstration was always the same. When you answered the door, a smiling man carrying a large case would announce, "Hi. I am your Fuller Brush Man and I have a gift for you." His gift was the Handy Brush and it was Fuller's promotional item to introduce you to their full line of brushes, and to get him in the door.

Almost as popular as The Fuller Brush Man was The Avon Lady, with her famous tag line: Ding, Dong, Avon Calling. Every few weeks The Avon Lady would drop off her latest catalog and deliver whatever lipstick and assorted cosmetics Mom had purchased during her previous visit.

Then there was the Biangaleen Man, selling Javelle Water, which was basically a bleach used to wash clothes. I know that Mom and my grandparents and aunts and uncles all bought Javelle, as did just about everyone else in the neighborhood.

Products weren't the only commodity sold door-to-door at the time. Every month, Mr. Slater, our neighbor from down the block, would show up with his little black book. He was a Metropolitan Life Insurance salesman, and would go to policyholders' homes to collect the monthly premium of $1 or $2. I remember Mom handing him a couple of singles and he would neatly note the entry in his book and give Mom a receipt. Try getting MetLife to do that today, and by the way, what do you think a premium of $1 or $2 a month would get you?

In addition to the salespeople who came to our door, there was another sales force, which drove down our street and drew your attention with a distinctive bell or song. These included Dugan Bros. Bakery, Ebinger's, fruit vendors, Chinese food trucks (that served Chow Mein in an edible noodle bowl) and the knife-sharpening man, all welcome traditions lost. The only street vendors that seem to have lasted are the ice-cream trucks. But their presence is nowhere near as significant now as the Good Humor and Bungalow Bar trucks were then. Just the mention of the names of those brands conjure up additional memories: The Good Humor napkin with the slot in the middle for the stick; the foot thick door of the refrigerated compartment; looking at the side of the truck wondering which flavor was on "special" for 5¢ less, hoping it was Toasted Almond, and the "No Riders" sign which was honored more in the breach than the observance. When it came to soft-serve ice cream, Mister Softee was the leading brand, but there was also the green Freezer Fresh truck, run by "Uncle Lenny." Mister Softee almost cost me my life as a young boy. I was sitting on the stoop of 718 Essex Street with Dad and Rob when the Mister Softee truck came down the block. I had always wanted a Humdinger, and had saved up enough to get one that day. After ordering the treat, I came around the front of the Mister Softee truck, where oncoming traffic could not see me, shielded by the truck. As I took one half step out into the street, a car whizzed by me. That freaked Dad out. The Humdinger went into the trash and my rear end received a royal beating!

It wasn't just ice cream trucks that got the kids' attention driving down the streets of Brooklyn. They actually brought amusement rides to us. The most popular was The Whip, but there was also The Half-Moon. Both were rides mounted on the back of a truck, contained in a wire mesh sort of cage.

The Internet is a lot quicker, but there was a definite romance to that door-to-door, face-to-face commerce that took place in my childhood.

CHAPTER 26

CARDBOARD CURRENCY

As a kid I remember hearing that money was the root of all evil, and yet I couldn't figure that out, since it seemed that everyone needed money to get some good things. Cars were good, because they got you to work and took the family on vacation, and the car and the vacation both cost money. Having a nice place to come home to and to share with your family were good things, and I know that every month my parents had to give money to their parents so that we could live there. So I wasn't too sold on this root of all evil theory. In fact, years later I would hear an adage that I think was more in line with how life seemed to be: Rich or poor, it's good to have money.

That being the case, I find it interesting how different societies treated different commodities as currency. We learned as children that Indians used beads, called wampum, as currency. We were taught that settlers in this country used fur skins as currency, and that colonists bartered different products, in lieu of a distinct currency system. Even today, countries trade in products and services, and certain products, like oil, are considered much dearer than others.

For a boy growing up in Brooklyn when I did, the commodity of choice was baseball cards, replaced from time to time by various inferior things like soda bottle caps. We carried baseball cards in our pockets by choice, and a clean, white handkerchief because Mom made us. Baseball cards were cool. They led to enjoyment in so many ways, some generated by the design chosen by Topps, the card of choice at that time. For instance, one year when the team name was written in white on the bottom of the card against a colored background, you and a friend would turn your cards over one card at a time alternating turns. If you turned over a card that matched the color of the card just turned over you won the pile. There we were gambling with cards as currency. Then there were the perennial forms of gambling with baseball cards, no matter what design: the most popular was pitching them against the school wall, like pitching pennies. Whoever got a card closest to the wall won all the cards tossed. If you got a "leaner", a card leaning up against the wall, you were almost sure to win, so everybody after you would shoot to knock down your card. The other all-time favorite was flipping cards. Two guys would flip and the guy who went last would have to match how the cards fell to the floor – either face up or face down. Every guy would try to come up with his own "formula" or style as to how to make a card land face up or face down.

Besides gambling with the cards, we would trade cards, like commodities traders. One thing every guy liked to do was to look through your friend's stack of baseball cards. You would hold the stack in one hand and peel off one card at a time, at a pretty good rate, saying "Need 'im" or "Got 'im" depending upon your own holdings. After you viewed your friend's stack of cards you would propose a trade. Just like trading someone five singles for a five dollar bill, you might see a guy trade five cards, of lesser pitchers, or journeyman players, for a bigger name player. Or you might see a blockbuster trade, like a Mickey Mantle for a Willie Mays, if you found two guys who were diehard Yankee and Giant fans, respectively. But the blockbuster trades were rare.

One ritual was going to the candy store and getting a new pack of cards. It was always great having someone give you a pack of cards, but it was really great picking out your own. It was very rare that you would pick a pack from the top. You figured that someone else left that pack there, and you would probably get Don Mossi and Jerry Lumpe, but never a Mantle or an Aaron or a Maris. When you finally selected your pack, you would open it and the sweet smell of that gum would almost force you to pop that stick of gum into your mouth. And as the sugar jolted into your system, every guy had his own way of looking at the cards he got. Just like poker players unfolding the cards dealt to them. Some guys fanned them out quickly looking for the rare superstar. Others peeked at them one card at a time, giving themselves enough time to say a Hail Mary or Our Father between cards, to coax the Lord into sending you one Mickey Mantle. The last thing you wanted was a manager or, God forbid, a checklist; what a waste of cardboard.

The cards also provided entertainment when you were alone. Guys would sort their cards by team, then they would resort them by number. We found many ways to enjoy the pictures of the guys we idolized and envied. Just about all of us had shoeboxes full of baseball cards that we cherished for their entertainment value, for their currency value, and for the dreams they let us have about one day having our face and name on one of those cards. While I agree with Tom Brokaw that our parents were the Greatest Generation, I know a lot of guys my age who find fault with our parents, especially their moms for eventually throwing out their baseball cards, cards that today would result in a windfall of actual currency.

One thing that is sad today is the absence of baseball cards in the playground. Cards are around. In fact, I am sure that many more new cards are sold today than when I was a kid. But it doesn't appear to me that anybody is enjoying any of them. Kids today open a baseball card pack like a surgeon: careful not to smudge a card, nor dare bend a corner for fear of lessening the investment value of a card. We would take all the non-stars and attach them to our bicycles so that as the wheel spokes passed over the card our bikes would sound like motorcycles. Today cards are collected merely as showpieces or investment items. Give me a five cent wax pack from 1960 with my piece of gum any day. By the way, if you have a 1965 Mel Stottlemyre, I'll trade you two Ron Hunts and a Jim Hickman.

CHAPTER 27

THE BB GUN

Dad was always bringing home different types of sporting goods, games and equipment to keep Rob and me active and out of trouble. He was all about keeping kids occupied and teaching us new things. One of the first things he did when we moved to 718 Essex was to finish off a portion of the basement into what he called a Rumpus Room. There we always had a safe, clean place to play that would be out of Mom's way in the apartment and we could rough it up, a little, without creating a problem.

With Dad everyday had to be a learning experience. If you went through a day without learning something it was a wasted day to Dad. It was not unusual for Dad to ask us "What did you learn today?" just before sending us off to bed. In order to insure success, Dad would furnish us with toys and games that were educational. I remember that: we each had a Gilbert's Chemistry Set; we shared a microscope with slides of spores and cells; Rob had an Erector Set and built a model of a see-through V-8 engine; we both always had model cars to build; and had a set of Remco Scientific Toys. I specifically remember the Remco Jet Propulsion Canister. The name of that seemed so futuristic. It turned out that the propulsion was provided by a balloon, which you inflated, placed on a plastic car, and then released the balloon. The escaping air propelled the car in the other direction. I'm not convinced that Wernher von Braun started that way.

One day Dad brought home two pairs of Everlast boxing gloves, one slightly larger (for Rob) than the other (for me). He said if Rob and I were going to fight (like most brothers do), and he couldn't stop us, he would show us the right way. He taught us how to wear them and how to use them, and let Rob and I proceed to have boxing matches in the Rumpus Room. No headgear – just boxing gloves. I remember they felt like they weighed a ton after a few minutes. I also remember how I could not believe how long three minutes was, as I waited for a bell to ring, while I did my own version of the Ali Shuffle trying to avoid getting the bejezzus beat out of me by Rob.

Dad also bought us a ping pong table, which was a little easier on my head and chest. I was the youngest, so I was the underdog, although playing against Rob and Dad made me a better player.

One of the other pieces of equipment that Dad brought home for Rob, since he was older, was a Daisy BB gun. Rob and I had always seen them advertised on the back covers of the comic books but never thought we would have one. Dad taught us how to load the BBs and how to prepare the gun to shoot and how to aim through the scope. He set up targets in the backyard, aiming away from people and other houses.

It didn't take long for the other kids on the block to get wind of Rob's BB gun. It was the only one on the block and it created quite a stir. Rob was our very own Davy Crockett. Several of us had the coon skin hat made famous by Disney. All of us knew the words to his Ballad, but none of us had a gun, except for Rob.

There wasn't much prey in East New York, but the kids on the block were all anxious for Rob to shoot something. With enough urging, Rob finally took aim at a Robin Red Breast sitting atop a fence post in Dad's garden. With a flick of the trigger a BB propelled toward the bird and knocked it off the post to the ground. As soon as it sunk in that the bird was dead, the sentiment of the group of kids changed. One of them yelled at Rob: "You killed a bird!" Then they all chimed in. Their thirst for Rob to pull the trigger was gone, replaced by a stunned disbelief that he had actually killed a bird. I felt bad for Rob and after that day the BB gun was only used for target practice when we were at a place with wide open spaces.

CHAPTER 28

CATHOLIC SCHOOL – PART V

EIGHTH GRADE – SISTER MARIE FONTBONNE

As a student who entered St. Gabriel's School in the first grade, the eighth grade was the anticipated pinnacle. We were the "seniors" of the school. We ruled the schoolyard. No older students could tell us what to do, or what not to do. The star roles in the Nativity play would belong to us.

Well, to paraphrase Robert Burns, the best laid plans of mice and men often go astray. During the summer of 1966, the stars aligned to insure that my Eighth Grade experience would be nothing like I imagined during my career as a St. Gabriel's student. Racial tensions, which had been escalating for some time, erupted during that summer, as evidenced by riots occurring throughout the country, and, of impact to me, right there in Bedford-Stuyvesant and East New York. The large number of relatives and close friends who lived on our block had decreased significantly. Uncle Sal, Aunt Jean and Aunt Angie moved to Merrick, Long Island in August of 1966. My grandparents announced they were selling 718 Essex Street and moved to Florida, and Aunt Mary and Uncle Dominick sold 720.

With all that was happening in the neighborhood, my parents decided it would be best if I spent the entire summer upstate. They rented a bungalow in Modena, New York, and for ten weeks I was removed from the heat, both physical and emotional, that existed in East New York in the summer of 1966.

By November of that year we had moved to Massapequa, but to avoid my having an unfinished symphony on my resume and my psyche, I commuted to Brooklyn, so that I could finish the Eighth Grade at St. Gabriel's and graduate in June 1967. But even the Eighth Grade was not as expected. My nun that year, Sister Marie Fontbonne, took ill and missed a great deal of the school year, probably the entire first half as I remember it. As a result there was no Nativity Play for us, as the school made due to cover for the ailing nun.

When she was due to return, several students, including me, decided to greet her with a play which we took from our English textbook. It was a drama about Louis Pasteur. My introduction to Broadway was halted in its infancy, when I flubbed one of my only lines. Commenting on Pasteur, I was supposed to say: "He cares more about the chicken in the laboratory than the chicken on his dinner plate" but I said: "He cares more about the chicken in the laboratory than the dinner on his chicken plate."

As a commuting student, with no family left in the neighborhood, the magic of East New York was starting to fade. I wasn't there on weekends, so my career as an altar boy was over, as was attending mass at the beautiful St. Gabriel's Church. There were no more stickball games in the streets, no more football games at Rich Field. Baseball practice under the el was gone, as were the nights on the stoop eating Italian ices.

All of it had happened, but now would only continue to exist in my mind.

EPILOGUE

I don't think the Brooklyn of my childhood can ever be recreated. We have changed too much as a society. We have changed too much as a world. That is not to say that children today or in the future cannot have great childhoods and great childhood memories, just that they will be different, much different than what I experienced.

The respective journeys of my grandparents and the investment, (physical, emotional and otherwise), that they made into the development of this country and their existence here, created within them a patriotism that was only capable of being created by the recipe of the life they endured.

My parents' generation, whose lives began in and around the time of the Great Depression, and whose teenage and young adult lives were stamped with the indelible impression of World War II, developed a unique appreciation for the liberty provided by this country. The losses they suffered, economic during the Depression, and maybe the loss of loved ones during the War, made them deeply grateful for whatever they had, and gave them a hunger to achieve the American dream through their work efforts.

Even though what they were able to provide for us was humble from an economic perspective, it was tremendous as a humanities lesson. Everything was rooted in family, not just on special occasions, but on an everyday basis. Your life was based around your family, and the love within that family. And from within that family and branching out to the community, all your actions were taught to be taken with respect: respect for others, respect for institutions, respect for authority, and respect for country.

We were awed by the ordinary; excited by the recurrence of annual customs. In fact, we were disappointed with the loss of the emotional anchor created by tradition if too much change or improvement took place. We didn't need spectacular. We needed steady. Our expectations weren't lowered. They were anchored. But we were encouraged to aim high, to succeed.

When I began writing this book, I wondered "What could have happened in the years between the age of four and thirteen, and how special a place could East New York, Brooklyn, have been to cause me to make so many mental trips back to a time and place so distant and different from my current surroundings?" I didn't know what the answer was but knew that it was magical.

Now that you have taken the journey with me, I hope I have been able to convey to you just how special it all was. With the benefit of having related my experiences to you, and taking a much closer look at all of it myself, I believe that I have identified the elements of what I have collectively referred to as magic. They are: humble beginnings, family, love, community, and respect.

No, the Brooklyn of my youth cannot be recreated because we are at a different point now, chronologically, technologically, and emotionally. I do all I can to keep the memory of it alive, as well as the memory of my relatives who provided those experiences. Hopefully, the very telling of this story will be helpful in that regard.

I hope you have enjoyed visiting my childhood, and if this story evoked any memories you would like to share please visit **www.storiesfromthestoop.com** and share your story there. Thanks for taking the trip with me. Now do me a favor and pass me an Eggplant Parmigiana sandwich.

CPSIA information can be obtained at www.ICGtesting.com
Printed in the USA
BVOW02*0114211015

423153BV00001B/3/P